BREAKING THE BANK

How the NIB scandal was exposed

George Lee   Charlie Bird

BLACKWATER PRESS

Editor

Aidan Culhane

Design & Layout

Paula Byrne

Cover Design

Liz Murphy

ISBN

1 841 313 777

© – 1998 George Lee and Charlie Bird

Produced in Ireland by
Blackwater Press
c/o Folens Publishers
8 Broomhill Business Park,
Tallaght, Dublin 24.

ACKNOWLEDGEMENTS

Special thanks to Ed Mulhall without whom this book would neither have been written nor published. Thanks also to Colm Connolly, Adrian Moynes, Liam Miller, Barry Linnane, Gerry Barry, Joe O'Brien, Kevin Rafter, Sean Whelan and Helen Whelan all of whom offered generous and helpful comments. We are indebted also to Aidan Culhane at Blackwater Press for his support, his patience, and for his skilful editing. The contribution of Mary Lee at all stages was invaluable.

CONTENTS

PREFACE

On 23 March 1998, the Irish Government went into emergency cabinet session as a result of our revelations of serious malpractice by National Irish Bank. It was an unprecedented response to a news exposé that had been two months in the making.

The country's fourth-largest bank had been caught stealing money from customer accounts. Confidence in the entire Irish banking system had been undermined. The image of bank managers as pillars of the community was shattered.

Bank customers everywhere began to fear that they too had been victims of similar malpractice. There was widespread disquiet and calls for a major shake-up in the way Irish banks were supervised.

Breaking The Bank is the story of how we uncovered the NIB scandal. It is our personal story. In telling it, our primary objective was to stick to the facts and to tell the full truth. We have written the book in the third person in a deliberate effort to make its subject matter accessible to as many people as possible. At all times, we were concerned to protect the identity of the people who put themselves at great risk to help us expose what went on at the bank. With this in mind, we have changed details which might tend to identify our sources. Some of the conversations we have included are based on the careful recollection of the participants and on our notes. Others come from verbatim transcripts.

Our work in exposing the malpractice in Irish banks has been followed up by other journalists such as Liam Collins in the *Sunday Independent*, Cliff Taylor in *The Irish Times*, Ursula Halligan in *Magill* and many others. In October 1998, we were declared Journalists of the Year for our work on this story. Yet for us, and for the others who took on the banks, the investigations are ongoing.

Charlie Bird
George Lee
November 1998

The First Few Days

7.15 P.M., THURSDAY, 15 JANUARY 1998

Charlie Bird stood at the corner of the bar in a busy city-centre pub. He had been there for half an hour and was well into his second pint of Guinness. In the time he had been there he had attracted plenty of glances from his fellow drinkers. It's hard to be anonymous in Dublin after spending 18 years on the television. The longer he waited, the more fidgety he became. It struck him that this may not be a good place to meet a potential source whom he had never met before.

In the past two days, in his search for a sympathetic ear, he had phoned several NIB insiders, none of whom were known to him. Although several had spoken over the phone, this was the first one prepared to entertain the notion of a face-to-face meeting. Bird had experienced a rush of excitement at the prospect of such a meeting and enthusiastically urged the man from the bank to choose the location. It was his idea to choose a packed bar.

Bird surveyed the pub for the umpteenth time. He had no idea what type of person to look out for. All he knew was that this potential source wasn't a woman, had sounded reticent on the phone, and said he would make the contact in the pub.

In an effort to be discreet, Bird had called himself Joe McGrath every time he rang NIB to try to speak with bank employees. Announcing his own name down the phone line to a receptionist, or secretary, or whoever answered the call would have set alarm bells ringing throughout the organisation. Conservative and secretive by their very nature, no bank wants to be on the receiving end of a call from an investigative journalist. As he sat there waiting anxiously for someone to walk up to him, Charlie Bird, alias Joe McGrath, ran over the sequence of events in his mind.

* * *

Four days previously, on Monday afternoon, he had received a phone call in the newsroom from a trade union activist. This activist told him he had a story which had the potential to be the poor man's version of the Ansbacher scandal. That Ansbacher scandal revolved around illicit payments into offshore bank accounts, systematic tax evasion, golden circles, and possible political corruption. It had been big news for months and had resulted in a Tribunal of Inquiry into the finances of former Taoiseach, Charles Haughey. A lot of very big names with very deep pockets were rumoured to be tied into the dealings. The result was enormous public outrage over the issues of tax evasion and offshore accounts.

The morning after receiving his phone call, Bird was sitting across a desk from the trade unionist in a city-centre location. The activist explained that he had been in possession of information relating to a National Irish Bank offshore investment scheme for about a year, but had been reluctant to pass on this information for fear of exposing the person who originally gave it to him.

However, now that so much time had passed and the Ansbacher controversy had become so big, the activist judged it was both safe and right to pass the information on to someone who would bring it into the public domain. That was why he had phoned Bird. He knew Bird was neither a financial whizz kid nor a banking guru. But he knew also that when he got a sniff of a good story the RTE man was like a terrier.

The trade unionist handed Bird a photocopied single sheet of paper with numbers scribbled all over it.

'Have you ever heard of Clerical Medical International or CMI for short?' he asked.

'No, what's that?'

'It's a fund management organisation with an office in the Isle of Man.'

The activist explained that a few years back, National Irish Bank linked up with CMI and established a scheme to help some NIB customers to put money offshore, technically. But the money stayed on deposit in the bank in numbered accounts. The customers were given the numbers and easy access to their money, but because technically the money was offshore, the Revenue Commissioners could never pry into it. The bank, the customer, and CMI all gained. The state and the ordinary taxpayer were the big losers.

The sheet of paper now in Bird's hand looked for all the world like gobbledegook. It contained 11 scribbled eight-digit numbers, two four-digit numbers with the letters PP before them, one with the prefix PA, four amounts ranging from £40,500 to £580,883, a few other scrawls, and then a key phrase '173 accounts altogether'.

'These account numbers and amounts were copied down from a computer screen in National Irish Bank over a year ago. They all refer to CMI accounts,' said the activist.

Handing over another seven sheets of paper he added: 'This here, is a detailed account statement for one particular customer.'

Bird looked at the seven new sheets of paper in front of him. They were typed out and looked official, but again they were photocopies. The new sheets contained the name and address of a man from a town in the west of Ireland and a detailed breakdown of investments he had under management by CMI.

'I gave these same pieces of information over to the Revenue Commissioners yesterday and I expect their investigation branch to make some inquiries,' said the activist. 'But as you know yourself, Charlie, the Revenue never make their investigations public. That's why I'm giving it all to you. This stuff really needs to be in the public domain.'

Bird returned to RTE about 20 minutes later. He had got some further clarifications from the activist who had even rung his original NIB informant twice to get more details while Bird was in his office. However, he still found it all quite confusing.

The language of investment banking didn't come easily to him. A list of scribbled numbers on a photocopied sheet of paper would never stand up in a court of law. The CMI printout for the man from the west of Ireland clearly showed his money was not on deposit in his local branch as had been described by the activist. Instead, it showed his £106,000 investment was split between the shares of leading Irish companies and offshore unit trust funds, managed by international fund managers including Fidelity, Fleming, Gartmore and CMI. Bird knew he would have to enlist some help if he was ever to get to the bottom of this story.

On arriving back to the newsroom, he rushed straight into the office of the Director of News, Ed Mulhall. He told him everything that had happened and asked who he could ask to help him.

George Lee, RTE's Economics Editor had some background in banking and investment. He had a very different approach and very different instincts to Bird. A trained economist who had taken to journalism, Lee, always on the lookout for a challenge, had changed jobs every two years or so in his early career. He could list the Central Bank, Riada Stockbrokers and *The Sunday Business Post* among his former employers. He had never worked with Bird before but Mulhall suggested they would make a good team. Bird didn't object.

Lee arrived in the newsroom half an hour later. 'Where were you?' asked Bird, not really looking for a response. 'I need you to work on a story with me. I've explained it all to Ed. Let's go for a coffee.'

* * *

Bird glanced at his watch again, 7.20. The NIB man should have been here 20 minutes ago. Maybe he wasn't going to show. Perhaps he was scared. Bird had told him on the phone that he was working on a story about the CMI investment scheme and that he had some bank documentation which appeared to back up the story.

The bank man had not passed any comment when the voice on the telephone told him he wasn't really Joe McGrath but was Charlie Bird instead. The reporter couldn't tell him where he got his name from, but asked if he had ever heard of the offshore investment scheme. The bank man said he knew what he was referring to all right and Bird had pressed him for a meeting. Eventually he agreed.

Now, however, as he looked down into his glass, Bird was getting a distinctly stood-up feeling. The sound of his mobile phone ringing gave him a start. It was the man from the bank, calling from his own mobile phone.

'Hello, Charlie?'

'Yeah, where are you?'

'I don't want to tell you Charlie, I'm scared. That CMI thing could cause big trouble for the bank. It's too dangerous.'

'Yeah I know, but can you still meet me?'

'No. I really didn't expect you to be here. I was convinced someone was setting me up.'

'Setting you up! What do you mean setting you up? Who'd be bothered doing that?'

'Charlie, NIB is getting worse day by day,' said the bank man. 'I thought someone from the bank was trying to trick me to see if I was prepared to tell bank secrets to a journalist. Obviously, I was wrong.'

Bird said nothing.

'Look, I'm really sorry for dragging you out tonight, but I'm afraid I can't meet you, I have too much to lose.' There was a nervousness in his voice now.

'But nobody will know, I swear I'll protect you. I'd never reveal your name, I'd go to jail first,' countered Bird, growing increasingly desperate.

'You've no idea how far these guys would go to protect themselves, Charlie. If they learned I helped you out, I'd never get a job in banking again, I can't take that chance. I'm really sorry. I'd better go now.'

'No, hold on,' Bird came back, 'do you know anybody else in the bank who might talk to me?'

'I can't, Charlie. It's too risky. If I had known it was really you who rang me today I'd never have come. I've got to go.'

The phone went dead. The television reporter desperately needed a source. Maybe some of those other calls Joe McGrath had put in would come up trumps. This wasn't the only promising one, yet this person had come so close. It was really frustrating.

Bird sat at the bar for a few more minutes thinking through the conversation he had just had with a man who only agreed to meet him because he thought it was a set-up.

What kind of a fellow would do that? he thought. Obviously he's very suspicious of the people he works for. He did say this CMI story would cause a lot of trouble for NIB. The poor man was so scared it was a set-up. He must have got quite a surprise when he saw it was for real.

Charlie Bird consoled himself with these thoughts as he finished his pint of Guinness. It was 7.30 when he walked out of the pub into the cold evening air.

* * *

George Lee sat at his desk and looked again at the list of numbers on the sheet of paper before him. The newsroom had quietened down considerably as it always did at this time every weekday. It was as good a time as any to review how much he knew.

Both he and Bird had pored over the hand-scrawled numbers on this photocopied page for almost three days. Obviously, whoever had scribbled this note had been in a big hurry. They pictured some senior bank employee with a conscience or a grudge, or both, sitting down one evening, punching the letters C M I into the bank computer, watching as the list of CMI numbered accounts scrolled up, and furiously scribbling some of them down before they were disturbed.

They felt lucky, and excited to be the recipients of that list even though it had taken a little time to decipher.

The handwritten list read as follows:

451520

81010212 — Finish - nil Balance $\frac{22}{11}$ /96

93007677   PP2228 £40·5k

73007812   PP2407 £92·2k

83008479

13687996

13014738   PAO125   £87921   Opened 12/11

23688356
93688674
13689034
33689352
93689417   Last   £580883

8 × 19 = 152
1 × 17   17
+ 4   4
_____   ___
           173   accounts altogether

Some things about the list were clear enough. The eight-digit figures down the left-hand side were the numbers for NIB accounts held in CMI's name in trust for NIB customers. The two PP and the one PA numbers were the personal portfolio code numbers associated with these accounts. These were given to the NIB customers by Clerical Medical International.

Obviously, the four amounts with the pound signs were the values of the relevant individual portfolios at the date the note was copied from the bank's computer. The sheet suggested that date was 22 November 1996, indicated by 22 over 11 over 96 in the upper right hand corner.

The note also suggested there was a wide range of investors involved in the scheme. The four amounts listed on the sheet ranged from as little as £40,000 to as much as £600,000. Apart from these four investors, there were 169 others involved, bringing the total to '173 accounts altogether.'

The average invested in the four accounts, for which amounts were listed, came to £200,000. Crudely extrapolating this figure over the remainder of the investors suggested to Lee that there was about £34 million invested in the CMI scheme in late 1996. Time would show that this crude estimate wasn't too far off the mark.

Both Lee and Bird had been told the investment scheme was set up in the early 1990s. Now the words 'opened 12/11' beside the sixth listed account was useful because it suggested the investment scheme was being marketed as recently as November 1996, the same month this reading was taken from the bank's computer. The implication was that the bank may still have been marketing the scheme.

The number at the top of the list '95 15 20' remained a mystery for now but Lee would learn later that it was the bank sorting code for the NIB head office branch at Wilton Terrace in Dublin into which all the CMI accounts were moved sometime in 1994.

Lee left the sheet of paper to one side and examined the seven-page CMI Personal Portfolio account statement for the man from the town in the west of Ireland.

It showed the investor had £106,000 under management. Twenty per cent of this was invested in Irish equities while the remaining 80 per cent was in a mix of offshore unit trust funds. The fact that none of his money was listed as being held in cash in Ireland, or more specifically lodged in a deposit account in his local branch of National Irish Bank, sat uncomfortably with the nice simple story he and Bird had been told by an NIB source the evening before. Lee thought through everything he had learned about the scheme over the past few days.

Contact with the original NIB source had finally been set up by the same trade union activist who had handed Bird these documents in the first place. Bird's constant phone calls and questioning had worn down the activist. He eventually tired of being the middle man and convinced his own NIB source to take phone calls directly from Bird.

That source outlined how the scheme was put into operation in the early 1990s at the prompting of a senior executive in the bank's financial services division.

Throughout the 1980s, like all other Irish banks, NIB was flush with accounts which had been deliberately set up to avoid the gaze of the Revenue Commissioners. These included illegal non-resident accounts and accounts in false names. In most cases, these accounts had been originally opened with at least the knowledge, and in many cases the assistance, of senior bank branch personnel.

But in the early 1990s the tax climate changed. The Revenue Commissioners and the Central Bank wanted the illegal non-resident accounts regularised. Like the other banks at the time, NIB was under pressure to clean up its act, but doing so carried risks.

A very wealthy group of depositors, those who got richer by avoiding their tax obligations, could decide to take their money elsewhere. If this were to happen it would not be good for business.

NIB was a small bank by international standards. It was a wholly-owned subsidiary of Australia's largest banking group, National Australia Bank. The Australians had bought it from The Midland Bank in 1986, changed its name from the Northern Bank to National Irish Bank and set about shaking up the Irish banking industry.

The bank from down under, however, expected a profitable return on its new investment. They knew the key to increasing profits was to grow the bank's customer base. Under Australian stewardship, NIB became arguably the most outwardly aggressive Irish bank in its pursuit of market share.

But NIB had to have money to lend out if it was to grab a larger share of the retail banking market. The cheapest and best way for any bank to acquire such money is to get it from depositors. The more they held in customer deposits the more profitable National Irish Bank was likely to be. Against this background, the offshore investment plan hatched in the financial services division of the bank had many attractions.

CMI would pay National Irish sizeable commissions for each investor they attracted to the scheme. The funds transferred to CMI could then be rapidly re-deposited back to the NIB branches from which they came so each branch's deposit base would remain intact. Depositors would surely be happy to have the ultimate cloak of anonymity, a numbered account which the Revenue Commissioners could never access. Arrangements could be put in place to ensure that the depositors could access their funds over the counter at their local NIB branch. Some of the bank's illegitimate non-resident accounts would be effectively 'cleaned up' as requested by the Central Bank. The CMI personal portfolio was a legitimate insurance-based investment product. Clerical Medical

International was a blue-chip company with a better credit rating than National Irish Bank itself. It had all the appearance of the ultimate solution. There could be winners all round.

Lee recalled the telephone conversation he had with the original NIB source the previous evening. He had been trying to figure how the CMI statement for the man from the west of Ireland had fitted in with his understanding of the scheme.

'This guy from the west of Ireland, his money wasn't on deposit in his local branch. The statement we have here, shows it was divided between various managed funds. There's nothing particularly odd about that.'

He was speaking to the NIB man on the phone but was looking directly at Bird who was sitting at the other side of the table to him nodding in agreement. They were in the office of the Managing Editor of News with the door closed.

'Oh well, that type of situation was the exception,' said the voice on the other end of the telephone line. 'Most of the investors had their money lodged back on deposit in their branch and they just came down to the bank and took it out over the counter. Sure I dealt with some of them myself.'

'So what do you think was the story with the guy from the west?'

'I know that sometime in 1994, head office decided this whole CMI thing was getting too messy. People were taking money out all over the place. A decision was taken to centralise all the CMI accounts in Dublin where they could be better controlled. It was always possible for the investors to choose not to leave their money in cash and I suppose when his money was moved to Dublin, your man from the west decided he wanted a better return than he was getting on deposit,' the voice explained.

'Would there be many like him?'

'There would probably have to be a few, but from what I remember, the vast majority of the investors left their money on deposit, especially in those early years. Interest rates here were very high in the early nineties after the currency crisis.'

'I see, but this statement for the investor from the west is of limited use to us at this stage. He could just claim he has his money invested in managed funds overseas which could be quite legitimate,' Lee went on. 'We really need a statement from someone who had their money put back on deposit in the bank.'

'I don't know where you'll get one. That was the only statement I could get my hands on,' replied the man on the phone.

'Listen, we don't doubt your story for a minute, but doing a story like this for TV can be quite tricky. We need more corroboration and probably more documentation. Have you any idea where we should try for those?'

'I don't know.'

'What about disgruntled employees? Presumably there are some people in dispute with the bank who just might feel strongly enough to talk to us.'

The voice on the phone came back. 'I'm sure there are. I know some people threatened the bank in the past, said they would expose all this offshore stuff.'

'Really?'

'Yeah, sure the scheme was dodgy as hell, and quite a few people know about it. There are a lot of pissed-off people in NIB. It's not like it used to be. People don't like the way the bank is being run these days. They just don't seem to care about anybody anymore.'

'Surely then, it shouldn't be too difficult to find someone who would talk.' Lee looked over the table at Bird as he said this. Bird was taking in every word.

The NIB source eventually came up with the names of some bank employees who had either had a run-in with their bosses in the past or who he knew were fed up with the way the bank was being managed. He didn't confine his list to those who were still in the bank but racked his brain and suggested others who had left the bank in the past few years. Lee scribbled down the names and made notes of where they might be contacted. He assured the source that none of those he named would ever find out it was him who had given their names to the two journalists.

As soon as that phone call ended, he sat there with Bird and reviewed the list of potential contacts they had just received. Bird wasted little time before starting to track them all down.

* * *

As he sat alone in the newsroom, mulling over this sequence of events, George Lee began to wonder how Bird's meeting in the pub had gone.

Did the man from the bank turn up and did he say anything useful? His phone rang. It was Bird in downbeat mood.

'How did you get on, Charlie? Did your man turn up?'

'He turned up all right, but he wouldn't meet me.'

'How do you know he turned up then?'

'He phoned me in the pub. Said he wasn't prepared to meet me. He thought it was all a set-up, that someone from the bank was trying to catch him out. Anyway, I'll tell you all about it in the morning, I'm going off for something to eat. Anything new there?'

'No, I'm still looking over the stuff we got the other day.'

'Okay so, we'll talk tomorrow, see you.'

* * *

Charlie Bird walked up Dawson Street and turned onto St Stephen's Green looking out for a restaurant. He was feeling a bit deflated having spent so much of the evening in that pub waiting for the man from the bank who turned up, but never met him. The two pints of Guinness he drank had gone down well, and the man from the bank had come close. Yet, he still had nothing to show for all the phone calls his alias, Joe McGrath, had made over the past 24 hours.

His mobile phone rang again and Bird stopped walking to answer it.

'Is that Charlie Bird?'

'Yes, who's this?'

'You rang me earlier today ... about the bank ... the investment scheme,' replied the voice.

He told Bird his name and said he would like to meet him. Bird's heart thumped, this could be the break he and Lee had been looking for.

'When can you meet me?'

'I could make it tomorrow morning,' came the reply.

'What time?'

'It would have to be very early. I don't want to be seen. I have to be in work for nine in the morning, so I can make it for about eight.'

'Okay. Where?' asked Bird.

'I don't know .... What about outside Bewley's in Grafton Street?'

'Okay, I'll be there. Are you sure you're going to turn up?'

'Don't worry, I'll be there,' said the voice. 'I'll see you then.'

'Right,' said Bird, and the phone went dead.

* * *

Bird tossed and turned in his sleep that night. The ups and downs of the day, combined with the excitement of the late phone call he received, had set his mind racing. He sensed this bank business could turn into a huge story. The thought that another source from the bank was about to meet him was reassuring. But would this source turn up, and what was he likely to be able to tell him?

* * *

Early the next morning, Charlie Bird paced up and down on the pavement outside Bewley's restaurant in Grafton Street. The restaurant may have been doing some business at this hour but the street itself was almost deserted. None of the shops were open yet, although the presence of one or two delivery trucks suggested it wouldn't be too long before the pace of activity picked up. The few pedestrians that were out and about were eyeing shop windows, on the lookout for last-minute bargains as the January sales drew to an end.

Bird looked at his watch. 7.55. The new man from the bank was due any minute. He looked up and down and paced about a bit more, wondering which direction this guy would come from and what he would look like. Then he heard the sound of his phone ringing and Bird immediately got a sinking feeling.

'Not again,' he thought as he pushed the answer button on his mobile.

'Charlie. It's me.' The voice from the evening before was instantly recognisable.

'Where are you. I'm at Bewley's waiting for you,' said Bird.

'I think it's too open, somebody is going to see me.'

Bird wished the man from the bank had thought of that before he chose the location in the first place.

'Can you think of anywhere else we can go?' he asked hopefully.

'I don't know .... It's hard to think,' came the reply.

'Well where are you now?'

'I don't want to say.'

Bird could have strangled him, but he kept any sense of annoyance out of his voice.

'How long have you got?' he asked the source, searching for a way forward in the conversation.

'I have to be in at nine ... have you got a car?'

'Yeah,' replied Bird, his expectation rising.

'Where is it?'

'It's parked outside the Passport Office in Molesworth Street.'

'Why don't I meet you there?'

'Okay .... It's a silver-coloured Opel Vectra.' He gave him the registration number. 'How soon can you get there?'

'Give me twenty minutes, Charlie. You sit in the car and I'll find you.'

The phone went dead.

The stroll over to Molesworth Street took just five minutes. Bird unlocked his Vectra and sat into the driver's seat. He felt certain this man from the bank would show up. For the next 15 minutes he sat in the car, searching the street with his eyes for anyone who looked like a banker. There were plenty of likely looking candidates. Men with briefcases scooted up and down Molesworth Street, heading towards the various insurance companies and investment houses located nearby.

As he scoured the street for his mystery banker, Bird paid little attention to the odd-looking man with the duffle bag who sauntered across from the pavement on the other side. He hardly even noticed as this duffle-bag man stopped 20 yards behind his Vectra and looked up and down before turning back towards where his car was parked. But when the front passenger door of his car was yanked opened and the man with the duffle bag sat in, Charlie Bird could barely contain his excitement.

The Duffle-bag Banker

He was nothing like the reporter expected. There was no briefcase, no umbrella, and no expensive suit. He just put his duffle bag on his lap, looked over at Bird, and nodded.

'Sorry about the messing. I think it's better here.'

During his 18 years in journalism Bird had met all sorts. As a Special Correspondent with a roving brief he couldn't afford to be choosy about who gave him information. Lots of strange people had sat in the seat where the banker sat now. The reporter had learned long ago that he could never judge how good or bad a source was likely to be by just looking at them.

'Thanks for coming anyway,' he said to the banker. 'Do you want me to move the car. I can drive around while we talk.'

'I think we're all right here,' came the reply.

That suited Bird. He didn't want to get stuck for too long with this banker. He could be a dud. The best way to find out was to get to the point as quickly as possible. He decided the best approach was to tell the banker all he knew.

The scheme, the deposits, the 173 accounts, the money over the counter. Could the man with the duffle bag tell him some more? To Bird's surprise he said he could, and he did.

The banker told him that it went on all over the country. He said he had seen how people were brought into the scheme. Certain members of the bank's Financial Advice and Services Division, FASD contracted branches. They were looking for customers with big deposits. The minimum amount required was £50,000. Many with accounts in false names or illegitimate non-resident accounts fell into this category.

Head office knew the identity of some of these people. They would have been noted when requests for credit on their behalf had been forwarded to Wilton Terrace in the past. Their hidden accounts would not normally be included on credit application forms but a detachable note was usually added. This note would point out that the net worth of the applicant was greater than that suggested by the form. It would refer to any non-resident or false-name account held on behalf of the customer. Obviously, customers of this type might be very amenable to the offshore scheme.

The banker shifted in his seat and cast a watchful eye up and down the street. Nobody seemed to be taking notice of the parked Opel Vectra with two men in the front.

He guessed that banking wasn't Bird's forte but somehow this made the banker feel more relaxed about talking to him. The reporter had interrupted him quite a few times looking for clarifications. He also furiously scribbled notes as the banker continued explaining.

A meeting was typically set up between a representative of FASD and the customer. This could take place at the local bank branch, or in the homes or offices of the potential investors. Sometimes the branch manager would make the introduction. Other times the investment advisers would go it alone.

The banker himself had been at some of the meetings. Customers he knew had been lured into the scheme. Others he knew had called it a rip-off. The administration fees were expensive. He confirmed that, in all the cases he was aware of, the money invested was lodged back on deposit in a numbered account in the NIB branch from which it had come. The rate of interest earned on deposit was the same as if it had never been 'transferred' offshore. He also confirmed that investors were given easy access to their money over the counter at their local NIB branch. When money was taken out over the counter, the bank had to inform CMI to make administrative adjustments at their end. It was all a bit crude, and it became quite tricky to manage. Eventually it was centralised in Dublin and tightened up a little. The investors, however, maintained easy access to their money.

As Bird continued his note-taking, all his doubts about the banker beside him melted away. He had confirmed everything the journalists understood about the story. He had a lot of experience of how NIB worked. Sure, he had some problem with the bank. Why else would he talk? There were a few of his bosses he particularly disliked. He had mentioned the bank strike of 1992 and the big change in atmosphere which resulted. But his motives for talking weren't really important. What mattered was that he had confirmed the story and had fleshed out the details.

It was now 8.40 a.m. The banker had been in the car for 25 minutes, a lot longer than either he or the reporter had expected. It was time to get moving. The street had got busier and he had to go to work.

'That's about it now, I'd better be off.' The banker was hugging his bag.

'Okay, and thanks for your help,' Bird replied. 'You've confirmed the story and given us lots more ... I'm just not sure how we can use it though. So far we only have one sheet of paper with account numbers on it. Our lawyers and editors will insist on more documents before we can report it.' Bird was thinking out loud but looking at the banker.

'Documents could be difficult to get.' The banker had a curious look on his face as he said this. Bird spotted it.

'You wouldn't know where we might get some, would you?'

The banker thought for a moment, then looked back at Bird.

'I'll think about it. I have your number.'

He studied the pavement on both sides of the street for familiar faces. When he saw there were none, the banker opened the door and gathered his duffle bag under his arm.

'See you,' he said.

He banged the door shut and walked briskly in the direction of Dawson Street. Thirty seconds later, he disappeared from view heading in the direction of Trinity College.

Bird sat for a moment tapping his steering wheel and considering his next move. Had he learned all he needed? Will that guy ever call again? He fingered his car phone, about to ring George Lee to talk it all through. A quick glance at his watch suggested it might be too early. He would go and have breakfast instead.

As he walked into Cunningham's Coffee Shop in Kildare Street, the Special Correspondent looked back across at the Dáil. He wondered what the TDs would say when this NIB story broke.

* * *

Lee sauntered through the wide RTE corridor which led to the edit suites at the back of the television building. He had a mobile phone stuck to his ear. At the other end of the line was a senior investment analyst he knew very well. He was reluctant to have conversations like this one while sitting at his desk. The newsroom was open-plan and at this hour of the morning it was noisy and crowded.

In hushed tones, he explained what he knew of the NIB scheme. His analyst friend could hardly believe it.

'Surely they didn't bring the money back into the bank. They must have been mad.'

'We were told that in the vast majority of cases that's exactly what they did,' Lee replied.

'But there would be no gain for the investors ... except to have a numbered account,' the analyst still sounded sceptical.

'That is the way it seems to us.'

'But those CMI products aren't cheap. How much did it cost the investors?' The analyst was all ears now.

'We haven't found that out yet.'

Lee found it reassuring that his friend on the phone was so amazed at the scheme. He knew there was nothing illegal about offshore investment products *per se*. But the reaction of the analysts reaffirmed that this was not your run-of-the-mill offshore scheme.

The analyst explained that investment products like CMI's are invariably 'wrapped around' a life assurance policy. This is done for tax efficiency and other reasons.

'One thing puzzles me,' said the expert on the phone line. 'How did the investors get access to their money?'

'They just went into their local NIB branch and took it out over the counter.'

'But that can't be true. Are you sure?'

'That's what we were told, by more than one source,' said Lee sounding confident.

The expert confided that he had never heard of a scheme like it before. He knew some of the financial sales force at NIB, but said a lot of them had moved on. He promised to check them out for the journalist. Perhaps one of them might be willing to talk. He did admit, however, that this was a long shot.

* * *

Later that morning, Bird and Lee reviewed all they knew with Ed Mulhall, the Director of News. They were confident now that the story was correct. It had been confirmed by two NIB insiders who had personal knowledge of the scheme. It had also been effectively confirmed by the demeanour of the man who had phoned Bird in the pub but was afraid to meet him. In addition, some of the further calls Bird and Lee made to other insiders had met with positive comments.

The journalists were so sure of their facts they were now bursting to tell the story. But exactly what level of corroboration did they need before RTE would give them the go-ahead? To answer this question, Mulhall called an editorial meeting. He phoned Eamon Kennedy, RTE's in-house solicitor, and roped him into the meeting.

Kennedy listened attentively to what the journalists had to say. The longer he listened the more disturbed he became. He expressed amazement at the circuitous way a deposit account in a false name could be transferred into a numbered account that the Revenue Commissioners could not access. The consequences of this story would be devastating for NIB. But if any of it was wrong, it could be devastating for RTE, as the bank would sue the station for millions.

Bird and Lee were delighted their lawyer was disturbed by the story. Eamon Kennedy had seen hundreds of big stories that were legally difficult to tell, eventually being broadcast by RTE. If NIB's offshore investment scheme disturbed him so much they must surely be on to a winner.

'So what do we need to tell this story?' Lee asked the lawyer.

'Proof,' came the reply.

'What kind of proof?' It was Bird this time.

'Documents, letters, memos. You really can't touch it until you have something in writing to back it all up.'

'I suppose our scribbled-out page doesn't count as proof.' This was more an assertion from Lee than a question.

'Afraid not,' said the lawyer.

'We have that statement from the man in Mayo. Is that any use?' Bird knew that it wasn't, but he asked the question anyway.

'No, it doesn't prove anything.'

The journalists and their boss sat talking to the lawyer for almost an hour. They were all in agreement about the importance of the story. The Ansbacher scandal had whetted the public's appetite for issues like this. It was decided that the pair should be left to dig deeper. Documents just had to be found. Perhaps one of the investors might talk. Then there were the people who marketed the scheme. Maybe, just maybe, one of them had become disgruntled with the bank and might consider talking. When Bird and Lee left Ed Mulhall's office later that morning they had a very clear view of what they needed to do.

* * *

'What time do you expect him in at ...? No, there's no message, I'll phone him back later ... Okay, thanks.'

Bird hung up the phone. He had tracked down the Mayo man with the £106,000 invested offshore. The CMI statement which the trade unionist had given him made no mention of the fact that he was a businessman from Castlebar. It was the original NIB source who had volunteered this piece of information. After that, it only required a quick look through the local phone book to track the man down.

The businessman, however, wouldn't arrive back until 7.00 that evening. That's what the young man who answered the call from a certain 'Joe McGrath' had just explained. Bird's adrenaline was pumping again.

Earlier he had phoned back the original NIB source to get more details about the investors. It was then he had learned the occupation of the man from Mayo. But he had pushed the banker hard. Could he not give him the names of any of the other individuals he knew in the scheme? The banker seemed genuine when he said he couldn't remember off the top of his head.

Bird had kept him on the phone a bit longer and finally a name tumbled out. It was the name of a wealthy businessman from a large provincial town. The banker couldn't remember how much he invested but he suggested it was quite a large sum. This particular businessman had plenty to spare.

It took Lee just seconds to guess the businessman's name. Bird had given him the clues over coffee in the RTE canteen hardly ten minutes after he got off the phone to the banker. This new investor was a real entrepreneur. He had started off as a retailer but now had many other business interests. He was also a former local politician. They decided Bird should contact him. It was 5.30 on that Friday evening when the businessman answered his phone.

'Hello, Charlie. What can I do for you?' The businessman sounded like he hadn't a care in the world.

Bird explained what he was investigating. He said he had learned the businessman himself was one of the investors in the NIB scheme. Without pausing for breath, the astute entrepreneur owned up. He said that, going back a few years, every second person had a non-resident bank account, including himself. When the tax laws got tougher it made sense to put money offshore.

'Sure aren't they all at it.' The businessman was referring to the information about offshore accounts and payments revealed by the Dunnes Stores Payments to Politicians Tribunal.

Bird told him the Revenue Commissioners had been given the same information he had originally received. However, he emphasised to the businessman that the Revenue didn't have his name, nor would he be passing it on to them. The businessman maintained his jovial demeanour.

'I suppose I'll have to pay all the taxes when I bring back the money. I've been thinking of bringing it back for a while. I'd better sort it out.'

The businessman then went on to confess that the illegitimate non-resident account he owned prior to the offshore scheme had been held in the Kilkenny branch of NIB. He said he would check his files to refresh his memory.

In all the time he spoke on the phone, the businessman never asked Bird who gave him his name. Being a man of the world he must have assumed the reporter would never tell him. Bird decided to ring him again.

* * *

Lee had spent the afternoon talking to sources in Dublin's investment community. He had been trying to establish how many experts knew of the NIB scheme. Were there any similar schemes available? He was careful not to give too many details to the people he spoke with.

He quickly established that the sale of CMI products by NIB was not much of a secret. However, nobody seemed to know how the scheme worked.

The analyst friend he had spoken to earlier phoned back. He had established that a relatively small number of NIB employees had worked in the area in the early nineties. It had taken a few phone calls to get all their names and the details of where they were now.

One had moved to a stockbrokers. Another had moved to a different area of the bank. A third had disappeared off the scene, gone abroad. Lee guessed that the stockbroker was unlikely to help. He was still involved in the same business, selling investment products to wealthy individuals. Surely he wouldn't risk his career by telling journalists about his last job. Dublin was too small a city for that.

The second banker would be a waste of time. He was obviously still set on a career in NIB. The chances of him spilling the beans were slim.

The fellow who had gone abroad might have some potential. He had obviously got fed up with the bank. Why else would he have packed in a promising career and a well-paid job, and disappeared? There must be some possibility that he could be convinced to talk. The big problem, however, was that nobody seemed to know exactly where he had gone. Tracking him down would be almost impossible.

Five minutes later, Lee was on the phone to another very well-informed industry source, a man with a very good grasp of offshore investments. He gave him some background on the senior executive in charge of NIB's financial services division.

The industry source had been aware of the CMI scheme at the time of its launch. He remembered that he had considered that the administrative charges were huge and said he considered them outrageous. According to his recollection, the investors had to pay almost ten per cent in charges to put their money into the scheme.

'And it wasn't even authorised,' he said.

'What do you mean?' asked Lee.

'I mean it wasn't legal to sell it. They needed approval from the Department of Industry and Commerce, or whatever it was then. They hadn't got that approval.'

'How come they needed approval?'

'CMI is based in the Isle of Man, and the Isle of Man is not part of the European Union. Under the Insurance Act, you can't sell an insurance product from an organisation based outside the EU without authorisation from the government. I know for a fact that NIB had no authorisation.'

The source went on to explain that the CMI link had proved very lucrative for National Irish Bank. He told about luxury incentive trips which CMI brought sales people on, but only when they achieved a very high level of sales. The trips were to places like Bangkok and Australia. All expenses were paid. First-class flights and hotels. Partners and spouses were included. He said he was aware that practically all NIB's sales staff had gone on such trips in the early to mid-nineties. He knew all their names.

* * *

Charlie Bird dialled the businessman in Castlebar again. It was 7.15 on that Friday evening. The same young man he had dealt with previously answered. Bird asked for the investor. Two minutes later, the receiver was picked up by a man with a Mayo accent. Satisfied he was the owner, Bird then told him he was investigating an offshore investment scheme operated by National Irish Bank.

'Your name has come up,' he said down the line.

'In what way has it come up?' asked the businessman. He was becoming more wary.

'We know you are in the scheme. We have copies of your statement from CMI. It shows you had one hundred and six thousand pounds invested in August 1996.'

There was silence at the end of the line.

'We also have a list of account numbers for other people,' added the reporter hoping the businessman would start talking.

'Where did you get it?' the businessman finally came back. Bird could tell he was shocked.

'I can't tell you that, but I can tell you that the Revenue Commissioners have the exact same information we have. They got it the same way as us.'

'Jesus!'

'Listen, we're not interested in exposing you, we just want to find out about the scheme, the way it was sold.' Bird was hoping to push the conversation along.

'I can't talk to you now.' There were hints of both nervousness and rage in the businessman's voice.

In the end, Bird wormed the businessman's home phone number out of him and arranged to ring him the next afternoon. Perhaps he might feel like talking by then.

The two reporters adjourned to the RTE social club. There, they reviewed all they had learned that day. The more they recounted their findings, the more amazed they became about how NIB operated its investment business. A lot of the jigsaw had fallen into place.

Yet, despite all of the information they had gleaned from their contacts, both journalists feared their story might never be told. They had no documentary evidence to support what they knew and without that evidence RTE would never consider exposing the bank.

* * *

The businessman was much more prepared when Bird phoned him the next day. The annoyance was still there in his voice. He urged the reporter to tell him again all that he knew of the scheme.

Bird asked him out straight if his money was hot. Had he been hiding it from the Revenue Commissioners? He answered that he had got it from America. But he wasn't convincing. Had he declared it for tax purposes? The reporter had pressed him again. No, the tax man knew nothing about it. That particular answer had pleased the reporter. It was further corroboration that someone with hot money was targeted for the scheme.

The conversation with the businessman went on for about 15 minutes. Charlie assured him again that he wouldn't be using his name. He also spurned new attempts by the businessman to discover how his name had come up in the first place.

When he was finished with the Castlebar businessman, the reporter made one more phone call. It was to the investor from the mid-west he had spoken with the previous evening. This time, however, the businessman was much more subdued. It was harder to get him to talk.

Having considered the issue all night, the businessman was now very annoyed with his bank. The money he invested, he said, was money he had for his children. In his view, the rate of return he achieved had been poor. Now someone had blown the whistle and landed him in trouble. He complained about the way the scheme had been operated, said it wasn't worth a curse. Before he signed off, he named the NIB investment executive who travelled to the branch in Kilkenny to talk him into the scheme. He also admitted again that the money he invested had never been taxed.

The Special Correspondent immediately relayed all this new information to Lee. The name of the NIB sales executive matched the details they had already learned. Both these investors had admitted their money had previously been lodged in illegitimate non-resident accounts. The two of them had also made it clear that executives from the bank had sought them out and invited them into the scheme. Everything now matched up with the story they first heard just four days before. Yet they still had no idea how to get their hands on hard evidence.

While Bird and Lee were thinking this over, the businessman from Castlebar was having thoughts of his own. He was still in deep shock that details of his NIB investment had fallen into the hands of two journalists from Dublin. He felt bad about that, but he was seething with anger that the Revenue Commissioners had been given the same details. If they proved him to be a tax dodger he could end up in jail. His business, his reputation, his lifestyle, everything could be ruined. Who was to blame?

Having thought it all through for a while, the businessman picked up his telephone and dialled a number he had found in the phone book. He told the person who answered to stay where he was. The businessman was coming to see him and he had better be there.

The Castlebar businessman jumped into his car and drove through the town. It didn't take him long to reach his destination. The man he had phoned was waiting in the doorway of his own home wearing a very serious expression on his face. He led the businessman into his sitting room and shut the door. He suspected there was big trouble brewing. After all, it wasn't often a local bank manager got a visit from an irate customer to his home at the weekend.

The bank manager sat listening to the businessman, the phone call from Charlie Bird, the Revenue Commissioners, the non-resident account, the offshore investments. The more he heard the more horrified he became. Half an hour later, he phoned his bosses in Dublin and told them the story of what the businessman had said.

The senior managers in Dublin had been aware that Bird had phoned some of their staff earlier that week. A few of the recipients of the Joe McGrath phone calls had reported the contact. But the managers were unaware, until now, of just how much the reporter had learned. They were also interested to hear that RTE now had two reporters working on the story. The threat to their bank was obviously much more serious than they had thought. They wondered where the RTE reporters were getting their information. The chase was about to begin.

The Proof

Bird had been sitting in his car for ten minutes and his windows were beginning to steam up. Although rush hour had long passed, there was still plenty of traffic milling about. Thankfully, the rain had held off and this made it easier to see the people moving about in the distance. He never thought the train station would look so pretty, flooded in lights.

The reporter had followed the instructions to the letter. 'Park outside the Eastern Health Board headquarters, opposite Heuston Station. Be there at eight and wait in your car.' Now, however, he was getting restless. Was this banker going to show up? Apart from dictating the time and the location, the source hadn't said much on the phone. As usual, Bird had jumped at the chance of the meeting.

Finally, at 8.06, he spotted the shadowy figure of a man in a raincoat coming out of the station. The figure stood for a moment examining his surroundings. He then waited for a clearance in the traffic before crossing briskly to where Bird's car was parked. Within seconds, the duffle-bag banker had opened the door of the Vectra and bundled himself and his booty into the front passenger seat for the second time in four days.

'We meet again,' Bird was the first to speak.

'Yeah, but at least it's dark this time,' the banker replied.

'And a quiet location too.'

He still didn't look any more like a banker than he had done three days before. But Bird didn't care about that. The banker had obviously spent the weekend considering last Friday's meeting. He must have come up with something new.

The reporter recounted his progress to date. He explained some of the phone calls Lee and himself had made. Everything they had learned was consistent with the story they were told on day one. But they were still desperately seeking the documents.

'I might be able to help,' said the banker, opening his duffle bag. 'I've been searching around.'

He took a thin folder out of his bag, extracted two pages from the folder, and held them in his hand.

'These,' he said slowly, 'refer to a wealthy businessman from the Cork region. He had more than half a million pounds stashed in NIB under a false name. In September of ninety-three he met with the branch manager from Mullingar and an investment adviser from the FASD division. They convinced him to invest in the CMI scheme. Five months later, however, the businessman had a change of heart. He decided to come clean and avail of the tax amnesty. He took his money back from CMI. When he discovered he had been charged £45,000 in charges for a five-month investment he had a really big row with the bank. Internal letters and memos were exchanged. I think they might be the proof yourself and George are looking for.'

'Forty-five thousand pounds ... for five months!' Bird was stunned. 'We heard it was expensive, but that's huge.'

'Here, you can read it yourself.' The banker gave Bird the two-page letter.

Fortunately the Vectra was parked right under a yellow streetlight which provided enough illumination to allow the reporter to read. He slowly read the letter.

It was typed on National Irish Bank headed notepaper. It came from Jim Delaney, the manager of the Mullingar branch of NIB and it was addressed to Dermot Boner, Head of Retail Banking at NIB. Just above Boner's name the words PRIVATE AND CONFIDENTIAL were written in capitals.

For the next five minutes the only sounds made in the car were caused by the rustle of paper and the gasps Bird uttered as he carefully consumed every word contained in the pages.

'... returned to the bank and invested on a term deposit.' He read this part out loud.

By the time the reporter was finished with the letter he was practically drooling for more. The banker was lapping it up.

'It gets even better,' he said with a smile.

The banker then retrieved another document from his folder. This time it was a three-page internal bank memo. It was addressed to Michael Keane, NIB's General Manager of Banking. The memo had been written by Dermot Boner, the recipient of the previous letter. Boner was telling Keane about the row with the businessman from the Cork region and the problem over the offshore fees. He also mentioned that NIB had been paid £18,000 by CMI for convincing its own customer to invest in the offshore scheme.

'This was how the row was eventually resolved.' The banker handed Bird the memo and then added, 'Keane and Boner were two of the most senior people in the bank, so you can be sure that knowledge of all this went to the very top.'

Bird read just as slowly as before and gasped audibly when he got to the part where it said NIB received a huge commission from CMI. He read the last line of the memo out loud.

'I know that we have a sum of the order of thirty million pounds in investments with CMI and I can foresee similar difficulties as this one in the years ahead, signed D Boner.'

Nothing was said as the reporter sat stunned by the contents of the memo he had just read. Surely this was all the evidence that would be needed to allow the story to be told. It was the banker who broke the silence.

'I have something else here which you might find useful.'

The reporter could hardly believe there was more.

He watched silently as the man in his passenger seat withdrew another small bundle from his folder and handed it to him.

'These are copies of lodgement and withdrawal slips related to the investment referred to in the memo you just read. What you might find interesting about them is that the businessman made the mistake of signing his real name on the bottom of one of the withdrawal slips. He then had to sign his false name beside it.'

Bird's heart pounded as he looked down at this latest batch of papers. There was a copy of the withdrawal slip for over half a million pounds. It had been filled out when the businessman closed his false-name account. Also included was a copy of the businessman's application for a bank draft for the money he had withdrawn. A copy of the actual bank draft, in the name of CMI, was also included.

The banker told Bird that he and Lee could use all the information contained in his documents. However, he insisted they couldn't be shown on television. After some further discussion, the man in the passenger seat began carefully putting his folder back into his duffle bag. The RTE reporter could not help wondering what other little gems the banker might have in his bag. Maybe, another day, he would be able to find out.

The banker looked at his watch. He said he had a train to catch. Seconds later, he hopped out of the Vectra and disappeared into Heuston Station. He had been in the car for 35 minutes.

* * *

Lee looked down at the bundle of papers. It had been half an hour since Bird had handed them to him. He couldn't believe that the evidence they needed could have fallen into their laps so easily. He looked over at Bird who sat sipping his coffee on the other side of the table. Excitement was written all over the older reporter's face.

Lee read the letter from the Mullingar branch of NIB for the third time:

National Irish Bank

A member of
National Australia Bank Group

Mullingar Branch

Austin Friars Street

Mullingar

Co. Westmeath

Tel (044) 40368, 42048

Fax (044) 42762

Date 28 April 1994

Dear Dermot,

In September 1993 [customer name] invested £558,569 with C.M.I. After C.M.I. had deducted their initial 3% the sum of £541,838 was returned to the bank and invested on a term deposit.

Prior to setting up the investment both Pat Cooney and myself had a number of meetings with [customer name and adviser] when all details relating to the possible investment were fully discussed.

Under the recent Tax Amnesty [customer name] decided to withdraw all his money from C.M.I., pay taxes due and reinvest the balance with the bank partly on Special Savings and the remainder on term deposit.

A difficulty has arisen is [sic] so far as C.M.I. before returning the funds deducted their full charges which would have been applicable over a five year period. These charges were in the region of £45K. At that time I spoke to FASD with a view to having said charges reduced for the fact CMI were managing the fund for circa five months and not five years as expected at the outset. I was informed that CMI would not under any circumstances compromise on the position.

Both [customer name and adviser] have recently contacted me expressing grave concern and objection to the level of charges applied by C.M.I. Despite the fact that full details were given to them day one regarding C.M.I. charges they cannot and will not accept the status quo.

What concerns me most is that [customer name] informs me that he was recently approached by AIB and B of I seeking his company business. I understand this approach was made solely as a result of the Jim Lacey saga. Obviously both of the said banks feel we are somewhat vulnerable at this time. [customer name] is adamant that a portion of the fee charged is refunded either by C.M.I. or the bank and he spoke in terms of £20K. Our failure to do so would urge him to reconsider the recent offers from AIB and Bank of Ireland. He also insisted that I bring this matter to your attention as being the right man to sort it out.

Dermot, I regret you have been dragged into this episode but I would greatly appreciate your guidance and support on the matter.

Yours sincerely,

J. Delaney.
Manager.

The letter was self-explanatory insofar as it dealt with the investor's concerns about the charges associated with his investment. Lee, however, had spotted something about the letter which wasn't so obvious.

He flicked over to the copy of the withdrawal slip filled out by the investor in August 1993. It was the withdrawal slip he had used to close his account in Kilkenny so he could transfer his money into the offshore scheme. He examined the two names the investor had signed on the bottom of the slip. The surname was the same in both cases but the Christian names were different. The official first names on the account being closed were Robert and Margaret. But the investor had first signed his true Christian name. He then had to sign beside it using the false name Robert.

The amount he was withdrawing was £539,014.39. The slip clearly displayed the stamp of a teller at the Rose Inn Street branch of NIB in Kilkenny. The date on the stamp was the same as the date at the top of the withdrawal slip, 25 August 1993.

'You know what this means, Charlie?'

'It means we have the evidence that the bank operated the offshore scheme,' Bird stated the obvious.

'That's not all,' said Lee. 'The tax amnesty was announced in May 1993. Anyone wishing to avail of it had to do so by the middle of January 1994. This letter and these slips imply the bank knowingly targeted someone five months after the amnesty was announced. They knew it was a false-name account held in a branch very far from where the customer operated his main business. The bank can't claim to be ignorant of his situation.

'This letter, and the withdrawal slips, show clearly that NIB knowingly invited a tax evader to put his money back on deposit in a numbered account in their bank at a time when it was clearly illegal to do so. NIB had a legal obligation to tell this type of investor to come clean. Yet, instead they went out of their way to encourage him to put his money into the scheme, right under the nose of the tax man.'

'And they took a big commission for doing so,' Bird butted in.

'Yes,' said Lee.

It is one thing to find a group of people using an investment vehicle to evade their tax responsibilities, it is quite another to find proof that a bank was actively encouraging them to do so. To have been behaving like this at the time of the tax amnesty makes matters even worse. NIB would find it very difficult to explain this away.

The two journalists had earlier spent some time considering how NIB might respond when news of their offshore scheme broke. They expected the bank would resort to the defence that they did not operate a scheme, but sold a legitimate investment product instead. They also expected the bank would deny they knew any of the investors were evading tax. The bank would probably try to claim that the tax affairs of the investors was a personal matter for those individuals and was not an issue which concerned the bank.

The evidence now in RTE's possession could blow all these claims out of the water. The tax amnesty had been the biggest thing on the personal finance agenda in August 1993. As far as the journalists were concerned, they had proof beyond doubt that NIB was guilty of a very serious offence.

Lee then turned his attention to the internal bank memo, sent to the NIB's General Manager from its Chief Manager of Retail Banking. He read it carefully for the third time.

Lee noted that according to the memorandum, the amount invested in the scheme by the businessman was £19,500 more than the total withdrawn from his false-name account. This gap had obviously been made up by funds he had on deposit elsewhere, most likely in Cork.

There were other aspects of the internal memorandum which struck the journalists. They were struck by how NIB had bent over backwards to appease the businessman for fear he might take his deposit elsewhere. They were struck also by the fact that NIB earned £18,000 for convincing its own customer to put money 'offshore,' despite holding on to the money themselves. With revenue like this to be had, the bank had a big incentive to push the scheme hard.

There was also the fact that CMI had charged the investor £45,000 for a five-month investment of just over half a million pounds. This fitted with the suggestions they had heard the previous week that the scheme was outrageously expensive. Who in their right mind would pay such a large fee to put their own money in the exact same type of bank account it was originally invested in, knowing it would earn the exact same rate of interest it was originally earning?

Another issue also struck them. It concerned NIB's investment and banking executives. How could they look someone in the eye and ask them to invest in a scheme which was so expensive to join and offered so little in return? A strong inference could be made that the NIB executives had a pretty good idea that the people they were inviting into the scheme were evading their taxes.

Although all of these issues kept the journalists talking for over an hour, there was one sentence from the memo which particularly impressed them. They had already learned that the bank had 173 CMI numbered accounts on their books in November 1996. Now they knew for a fact that NIB had £30 million of investments with CMI in August 1994.

The time had arrived for the journalists to start seeking answers from the bank.

* * *

'Can you put me through to Philip Halpin's office? ... It's Charlie Bird from RTE ... Hello, can I speak with Philip Halpin please? ... Charlie Bird ... I have a very important letter to send him and it's critically important that he is there to receive it ... It's about a news story concerning the bank which RTE is planning to broadcast ... Can I be sure he'll get it? ... Okay I'm sending it over immediately by courier ... Bye.'

Bird put down the phone, confident that the secretary to NIB's Chief Operations Officer would hand his letter directly to Philip Halpin as soon as she received it. Seconds later, a motorcycle courier was dispatched from RTE with a letter the journalists knew was going to rattle the bank. The letter read as follows:

Dear Mr. Halpin,

RTE News is working on a story for transmission during tomorrow night's bulletins, Wednesday 21st January, on National Irish Bank's involvement with Clerical Medical Insurance based in the Isle of Man, London and New York.

Could you please tell us when the Financial Advice and Services Division of NIB began directing its customers to Clerical Medical Insurance?

RTE News has been reliably informed that a number of customers with NIB, during the early nineties were encouraged to move their non-residential accounts and other accounts with sensitive monies in them into CMI personal portfolios.

Is this correct, and if so, how many customers were encouraged to move their business off shore to CMI in the Isle of Man, London or New York?

RTE also has information to suggest that the funds held in the non-residential accounts and accounts with sensitive monies when closed, within days, were re-lodged into National Irish Branches under CMI personal portfolios. Is this correct?

RTE News has information to suggest that at one stage in 1994 National Irish Bank held CMI personal portfolios for Irish residents in excess of 25 million pounds. Is this correct?

RTE News has also been informed that these CMI accounts were moved from the various branches around the country to the Financial Advice and Services Division at Wilton Terrace. Is this correct and if so, when did this happen?

RTE News has learned that in 1996 there was somewhere in excess of 50 million pounds in these CMI personal portfolio accounts, being held at Wilton Terrace. Is this correct?

RTE News has learned that a number of NIB representatives and their spouses from the Financial Advice and Services Division were brought by CMI to an international conference in Australia, as a thank you for the amount of business which they obtained for CMI. Is this correct?

Did Beverly Cooper Flynn handle the CMI accounts? Would she have been fully aware of the procedures involved in the transfer of the monies from NIB branches to CMI and did she avail of the trip to Australia?

RTE News understands that when a customer moved to CMI, NIB received a commission somewhere between 3% and 5% of the sum invested with CMI. Is this correct?

RTE News also understands that CMI put the money back on deposit with NIB. Is this correct?

Why did you advise clients to invest in CMI?

Why did you advise them to move to offshore accounts outside of Ireland?

What classes of NIB customers did you approach suggesting CMI investments?

Did you continue to approach this type of customer to move their business to CMI after the most recent tax amnesty?

Did you feel NIB's marketing of this type of products to people who held non-residential accounts or accounts with sensitive monies in them, was ill-advised and allowed a situation to continue whereby individuals did not comply with their obligations under income tax and general laws in this country?

RTE understands that the initiative for the arrangement with CMI came from Financial Advice and Services Division of NIB and was approved at Chief Executive level within the Bank. Is this correct?

When the tax amnesty for offshore accounts was introduced, did the Bank ensure that the clients with the sensitive monies held offshore, avail of the amnesty?

Is NIB satisfied that the operation of these accounts was fully compliant with Irish Tax Law, Exchange Control and Banking Regulations?

I would be obliged if you could provide answers to these questions as soon as possible in order to allow us to transmit a fair and accurate report on this issue.

Yours sincerely,

Charlie Bird
Special Correspondent
RTE News

The two reporters had earlier been locked away with Ed Mulhall and Eamon Kennedy for two and a half hours. Collectively, they had reviewed all the evidence and the facts of the story. Lunchtime had come and gone but nobody in the room had noticed.

As Director of News, Ed Mulhall was adamant that the bank would have to be treated fairly. NIB must be given the chance to tell its side of the story. Mulhall insisted that the requirements laid down in the Broadcasting Act for balance and fairness should be observed.

But how much time should the journalists allow for the bank to respond? At least 24 hours was the verdict, although nobody in the room felt confident the story could be broadcast that soon.

It had not taken long for the questions to the bank to be typed up. Everyone in the room had given suggestions and Bird had signed the letter.

'Maybe I'll sign Joe McGrath,' he joked. 'Do you think Philip Halpin would know who that was?'

His question didn't require an answer because the four of them knew Bird's cover had already been blown.

The Bank Responds

A letter arrived addressed to the Director of News and marked urgent. This was the second communication which had come from the bank in the space of three hours.

The first statement had been greeted with derision by the two journalists. It had consisted only of four sentences about CMI being a reputable institution and about NIB selling CMI products. It said nothing about non-resident accounts, tax evasion or commissions.

From the perspective of the journalists, it had been a useless statement. The bank had deliberately avoided the issues raised in Bird's letter of the previous day.

This letter to the Director of News, however, was a very different type of communication indeed. For starters, it came from NIB's solicitors, Matheson Ormsby Prentice. Second, it was of considerable length. Third, and most importantly, it carried a statement which stopped the journalists in their tracks seconds after it arrived in the newsroom. The letter from NIB's solicitors read as follows:

Dear Sirs,

We act on behalf of National Irish Bank and have been instructed to respond to your letter of the 20th January 1998 delivered to our clients at approximately 4.00 pm yesterday afternoon.

The letter clearly accuses National Irish Bank ("the Bank") of being actively engaged in tax evasion. The Bank does not condone tax evasion and our investigation in the very brief time available has found no evidence to sustain the very serious allegation Mr. Bird makes. We would ask Mr. Bird to make available to us any details he has that would be material to our on-going investigations.

The Bank openly marketed to its customer [sic] Clerical Medical International (CMI) personal portfolios. There is nothing illegal in investing in such portfolios. From the customer's point of view there is no tax implication during the life of the CMI personal portfolio investment. On realisation there may be tax implications but that is a matter which is governed by the performance of the investment and the investor's personal tax situation.

CMI, in common with other investment product vendors, has assets to invest. In consideration of the business introduced to them, they would place deposits with the Bank. Accordingly, on occasion, CMI would invest some or all of CMI personal portfolio in National Irish Bank deposits. At all material times deposits invested by CMI and the accruals thereon were the property and responsibility of CMI and not of CMI customers.

The Bank has learned that Mr. Bird is in possession of confidential information relating to the business of the Bank and its individual customers. His information clearly enjoys a quality of confidence which protects its disclosure to third parties. It is clear that Mr. Bird would have been aware of the confidential nature of the information and in fact that its disclosure to him was in breach of both the quality of confidence and the duties of confidence owed by the persons who had the information. Any publication of such confidential information which will include, but is not limited to, the names of the account holders and the banking arrangements they had or maintained with the Bank or investments they have made with CMI or others, is a wrongful action on the part of Mr. Bird and RTE.

It is untenable that the Bank should be informed of Mr. Bird's allegations late on the 20th January 1998 with a threat of publication the following day.

There can be no justification for such precipitous behaviour but the desire of RTE to irresponsibly damage the Bank. We trust it is not too late to try and avert the damage that will be caused and has been caused.

Yours faithfully,

Matheson Ormsby Prentice.

Bird and Lee read the legal letter carefully. The bank's complaint that it didn't have enough time to investigate the 'serious allegations' made by RTE came as no surprise. The journalists figured NIB would have made the same complaint if they had set a two-week deadline for a response.

The request for RTE's information to help the bank with its own investigations, was also par for the course. They would have no hope of getting any assistance from the journalists at this early stage.

Bird and Lee had also anticipated the NIB claim that there was nothing illegal about selling CMI investment products. They suspected this was untrue however, especially if they could prove that NIB had not been properly authorised to sell CMI products in the Irish Republic.

NIB's claim that the personal tax implications of the scheme had nothing to do with the bank, but was an issue for the investors themselves, was exactly what the reporters had predicted the bank would say. George believed this claim could also turn out to be untrue. He had checked through tax legislation and learned it had been a criminal offence since 1982 for anyone to knowingly assist a person to evade their taxes. If the evidence they had in their possession was anything to go by, then the investors were not the only ones who had fallen foul of the tax laws. NIB itself could have questions to answer.

The fourth paragraph of the solicitor's letter however, caused a lot of difficulty. When they read it, the journalists were mindful that this communication had come from one of the top legal practices in Dublin. But the fourth paragraph of their letter implied that National Irish Bank had nothing to do with the decision to re-lodge investor funds back into the NIB branches from which they originated.

Instead, the bank, through Matheson Ormsby Prentice, were clearly suggesting that this decision was taken by the Isle-of-Man-based CMI, acting alone. They even insinuated that when CMI did lodge money to the bank, they did so as a type of pay-off for all the business NIB was sending their way.

The reporters recognised immediately that if this suggestion turned out to be true, it would dilute the seriousness of their story. They would not be able to claim the bank had operated an illicit scheme. All they would be able to say about NIB was that it sold CMI investment products to their customers. This was precisely what the useless four-sentence statement they had received earlier from the bank had said. The letter from NIB's solicitors had effectively taken the bank itself out of the story.

What was left was a tale about a few businessmen from different parts of the country using offshore investments to evade tax. To make matters worse, the journalists only had the names of two of the businessmen currently involved.

In the wake of the Ansbacher controversy, this wouldn't be much of a scandal. CMI operated outside the jurisdiction so there would be little the government could do in response.

The story which Bird and Lee believed they had uncovered was that it was NIB who ensured the money invested in the scheme was brought back to its branches. This was the core of the scandal. If this couldn't be proved, the whole story would fall apart. Now they had one of the most reputable firms of solicitors in the country telling them in writing that it just wasn't true. The pair were devastated.

Lee picked up the bank's earlier statement and read it again. This time however, he treated it with a bit more respect. The statement had been delivered at a quarter to five that Wednesday evening. It read as follows:

COMPANY STATEMENT

Clerical Medical International (CMI) is a well established and respected international financial institution. Its products are available from National Irish Bank and other financial intermediaries. These products are well regulated and are openly marketed by National Irish. National Irish has sold CMI products for many years. National Irish acts as agent for a wide variety of financial products available from Irish and international institutions.

ENDS

21 January 1998

The combination of the solicitors' claim that CMI acted alone when placing deposits with the bank and this short press release from the NIB was very effective. The reporters had been well and truly stumped. They would now be unable to lay a glove on National Irish Bank. Everything they had learned and even the reliability of the bankers who had given them assistance would have to be questioned.

* * *

The atmosphere in Ed Mulhall's office early the next day was downbeat. Eamon Kennedy had arranged for a consultation with RTE's senior counsel, Kevin Feeney. The objective was to run through all the evidence amassed by Bird and Lee and advise on what they could and could not say in a broadcast.

This session had been arranged two days previously, long before the letter from Matheson Ormsby Prentice had stopped the journalists in their tracks. Now the objective was to see what type of a story could be salvaged if the bank had to be written out.

The journalists themselves had each spent over an hour on their phones prior to the meeting with their legal advisers. They had been trying desperately to retrace all they had learned to see where they could have gone wrong. They had spoken with almost all of their contacts again. They each found that their sources were sticking to the stories they had recounted before.

The bankers they phoned were particularly stunned at the suggestion that legally NIB may have had nothing to do with CMI's decision to lodge money on deposit in the bank. As bankers, they said, they found it hard to believe. All had been at meetings between investors and the bank's FASD representatives. They swore there was never any doubt it was the investors' money, not some independent CMI fund, which was put back on deposit in the NIB branches.

Although such re-affirmations were comforting, they did little to ease the plight of the journalists. Neither Bird nor Lee would ever be able to convince RTE's lawyers that what had been said in the letter from the bank's solicitors was untrue solely on the basis of what they had been told by anonymous sources. Experience had taught them that lawyers were likely to be more interested in what they could prove in a court of law than in what reporters wanted them to believe.

Reluctantly, Bird and Lee were coming to the realisation that, to all intents and purposes, their story was scuppered.

Bird stayed at his desk talking on the phone as Lee joined the meeting in Ed Mulhall's office. Mulhall and himself, along with their solicitor, proceeded to explain the whole story to the RTE barrister. They told him everything, the apparent targeting of customers with sensitive monies, the closing of illegal non-resident accounts, the circuitous flow of deposits back to the bank. They left nothing out.

When they had finished explaining the details of the story they originally wanted to tell, Lee handed the documentary evidence over to the barrister. Everyone stayed quiet as Kevin Feeney read the contents of the letter written by the bank manager from Mullingar. They were equally silent when he moved on to the internal memo from Boner.

Feeney was thoroughly impressed. Everything seemed to fit into place.

'Have you contacted the bank?' Feeney then asked.

'We have, we sent them a letter on Tuesday,' Lee replied.

'What did they say?'

'They said they had nothing to do with the decision to re-lodge the money back to the bank. They implied CMI was totally responsible.'

'Oh,' was all the barrister could say as the implications of this new factor rapidly sunk in.

'They used a solicitor's letter to gives us that news,' said Lee. 'Obviously, it has caused us some problems.'

The RTE barrister didn't comment. Lee went on to explain that Bird and himself had gone back to their sources to re-check their facts. He said that he and Bird were finding it difficult to accept that NIB was not responsible for the circuitous flow of deposits. To his relief, everyone in the room agreed with this point of view, even the barrister. However, they also agreed that the investigation was stuck for the moment. NIB would have to be written out of the story for now.

They had started picking through the facts once again to see how much of a story was left when Bird burst into the room.

'I just don't understand it .... He was on about wrap arounds, and life policies. He was getting very technical. He has me all confused.' The reporter was very worked up.

'What are you on about Charlie?' Lee was surprised by his colleague's distress.

'Yer man from CMI .... He said they didn't have anything to do with it.'

'What exactly did he say?'

'I really don't know any more, it was all financial jargon. But something sounds wrong. You're going to have to ring him. At least you might be able to understand what he says.' Bird was still pacing about.

'Who did you speak to?'

'That David Shelton chap we both rang before.'

'Did you tell him what NIB said?' Lee asked the question, but RTE's solicitor, barrister, and Director of News were all bursting to ask it as well.

'Yeah, I read him their solicitor's letter.'

'And what did he say?'

'He said it was wrong.'

* * *

Three minutes later, Lee went to his desk and dialled the CMI office in Bristol. He eventually got David Shelton on the phone. The CMI communications officer explained that the investment bonds which NIB sold to their customers were Personal Portfolio bonds. He said the investors who purchased these bonds had to nominate an institution or person who would advise them on how their funds should be invested. The only thing CMI offered the purchaser of the bond was a facility for putting money offshore.

The decision on how the funds were actually invested depended totally on the relationship between the investor and his investment manager. He said NIB acted as the investment manager for all of its customers. This meant it was NIB who decided, in conjunction with its customers, exactly how the money should be invested.

CMI, he insisted, never gave any advice to the purchaser of a Personal Portfolio bond in relation to the management of their funds.

There was a hint of annoyance in Shelton's tone as he dismissed the letter sent to RTE by NIB's solicitor the previous evening.

'You can quote me on this,' he said. 'The Personal Portfolio product sold to NIB customers was termed "whole of life". It was not a fixed-term investment. It could effectively run until the investor died. However, there was no lock-in period. The investors could withdraw some, or all, of their money at any time. Where the money was invested was entirely a matter decided between the investor and National Irish Bank.'

Shelton put extra emphasis on the next bit.

'Categorically no assets were ever invested by CMI in National Irish Bank "in consideration" of the business introduced by the bank. CMI makes its own investment decisions completely independently of its products and the distribution of its products.'

This was a categorical dismissal of NIB's defence.

Lee read the entire quote back to him twice to ensure the CMI communications man in Bristol was happy with what he had said. Each time he read it, the CMI executive became more emphatic that his quote could be used.

* * *

The mood of the meeting soared when Lee arrived back with the quote. The bank's attempt to mislead the journalists had been exposed. The useless four-sentence statement followed by the letter from the solicitors had bought NIB some time. But now the two journalists were back on the trail. They had learned an important lesson. They would never be able to trust the word of the fourth-largest bank in the country.

The journalists and their lawyers got back down to work. A detailed review took place of what could be proven in court. This was the yardstick against which everything had to be measured. Nothing that was hearsay could be allowed in a broadcast.

It would take time to work on the script. Television graphics would have to be ordered and cameramen sent out to film the NIB headquarters. The scandal of the story would undoubtedly cause a big embarrassment. One little mistake and the damages could run into millions.

* * *

It took another day and a half before the story about NIB's offshore investment scheme was ready for broadcast. Bird and Lee had to spend hours drafting and redrafting their script. The imposition of legal constraints meant they had to settle for a slightly technical presentation of the facts.

The tax man had received the same original details as Bird and Lee. A few calls to the Revenue Commissioners confirmed they would be investigating all aspects of the bank. This gave the reporters an important new peg for their story.

When Bryan Dobson introduced the early evening news on Friday 23 January his third headline read:

'Multi-million pound offshore investments to be examined by the Revenue Commissioners.'

Five minutes later he introduced the fruits of two weeks of journalistic investigation.

'RTE news has learned exclusively that the Revenue Commissioners have been provided with details of an offshore investment scheme operated by National Irish Bank. RTE has learned that some account holders have used the scheme to avoid or evade tax. It is believed that the Revenue Commissioners will be examining the information which has been passed on to them. This report is from our Special Correspondent Charlie Bird and our Economics Editor George Lee ....'

It had taken quite a long time to craft this introduction and every syllable had to be approved by the Director of News and RTE's lawyers. The television report, voiced by Bird, ran as follows:

'Prior to 1994, representatives of the National Irish Bank gathered information in relation to about 180 of its customers throughout the country. These included people who held non-resident accounts,

accounts in false names, and accounts with funds which had not been disclosed to the Revenue Commissioners .... The money was handed over by bank draft to Clerical Medical International in the Isle of Man. Within days, this money, minus the set-up charges, came back to the National Irish Bank .... The bank was able to retain on its balance sheet most of the funds belonging to the holders of the accounts involved and also earned sizeable commissions from Clerical Medical International for selling the bonds ... was paid close to £20,000 in commission for persuading a customer to invest half a million pounds ... in excess of 150 National Irish Bank customers accepted the bank's invitation to invest in the CMI bonds ... a customer cashed in his bond to avail of the tax amnesty in early 1994 ... in August 1994 the total amount still invested through the scheme was of the order of £30 million .... National Irish Bank has told RTE that it does not condone tax evasion and following our enquiries are conducting an ongoing investigation.'

* * *

Far from the newsroom, in several parts of the country, the secret contributors to the RTE exposé carried on as normal. Their day at their offices had just come to an end. All knew the story was due to break. Yet none made an attempt to catch the *Six One* bulletin. To do so would be out of the ordinary for executives who normally drive home at this hour. All were convinced that their friends and colleagues were oblivious to their involvement and they wanted to keep it that way. Rushing into some pub to catch the early evening news could signal a prior knowledge of the bulletin. There was little point in offering such a hostage to fortune. They could catch the television news later at home.

If they had turned on their car radios as they drove home they would have heard George Lee deliver a short version of the story. He had recorded it for the top of the 6.00 radio bulletin.

As the secret contributors followed their usual routines, they wondered what impact their revelations might have. Like the journalists they had assisted, they expected it to make a splash. But they could never have anticipated how big that splash was going to be.

All the contributors were aware that passing on sensitive banking information to journalists could be explosive. They knew they had taken great personal risks to help the reporters with their story. In parked cars, hotel rooms, or just down the phone, they had told how it worked. They explained the practices they engaged in as the bank which demanded their loyalty became increasingly ruthless in its pursuit of profits. Most people think of bankers as a risk-averse bunch, instilled with conservatism and loyalty to their employers but loyalty to the bank had long since ceased to occupy a priority place in their feelings. Disgust and anger had become the dominant attitudes. As far as the journalistic sources were concerned, the Australian-owned bank had a lot to answer for.

National Irish Bank will always believe the informants who assisted the RTE investigators are guilty of some crime. The bank insists they stole documents and broke the code of confidentiality so sacred to bankers. The bank had publicly threatened to use the financial resources of the wealthy Australians to catch and pursue anyone who was passing on information or documentation. The impact of such a threat would have scared off many a journalistic source. But Bird and Lee had been lucky. They hit on a few diehards incensed enough by the way NIB ran its operations to take the risk of consorting with them in the public interest.

* * *

For the following two and a half hours Bird and Lee hung around the RTE newsroom waiting for the bank to react. If NIB said anything, the reporters would have an obligation to mention it in their report for the *9.00 News*. They both figured the bank would have to respond because to do nothing would be interpreted as an admission of guilt. But would NIB come out with a legal writ or a straightforward statement this time? The 9.00 deadline was almost upon them when they learned that a fax was on its way through.

When the journalists picked up the fax they could hardly believe what they saw. It was a short simple statement as follows:

STATEMENT

National Irish Bank is carrying on an internal investigation into the allegations broadcast on television this evening. The investigation is being processed rigorously to determine the facts of the situation. The allegations are of a most serious nature and in contravention of the banks' policies. The Bank does not condone tax evasion. The Bank will co-operate fully with the Revenue Commissioners and any other regulatory authorities in their investigations.

23rd January 1998

The reporters were thrilled. There was no threat of legal action and no hint of a lie.

'Hey Charlie, they must be getting to like us,' said Lee.

'Why's that?'

'Because they've become more communicative. Look, they've written five sentences for us this time.'

Bird chuckled then headed off downstairs with a cameraman. It only took a few minutes to incorporate the latest NIB statement into a new sign-off to the report for the main evening news.

The Tallaght Interview

Bird and Lee walked into the press gallery in the Dáil. They wanted to hear for themselves what the Minister for Finance had to say about NIB. Michael Noonan, the finance spokesman for Fine Gael, the largest opposition party in the Dáil, had tabled a formal question to the minister for the adjournment debate.

Noonan's question was 'to ask the Minister for Finance if he has established whether certain offshore accounts in National Irish Bank were used for the purpose of tax evasion ... and if he will make a statement on the matter.'

In his answer, McCreevy confirmed that the Revenue Commissioners were 'examining urgently all the tax issues involved.' He added that 'all necessary action will be taken by the Revenue to deal with whatever tax consequences emerge.'

The minister also said he had written to the Governor of the Central Bank on the Monday after the story broke. He had asked the Governor to report to him on the issues raised by the offshore scheme. 'The Central Bank is examining the possible exchange control implications of any transactions involving offshore accounts, but I should point out,' added the minister, 'that such controls expired on 31 December 1992.'

McCreevy told the Dáil that the Minister for Science, Technology and Commerce, Mr Noel Treacy TD, who has responsibility for the regulation of the insurance sector, was also playing a role. He said Treacy had written to National Irish Bank on the previous Tuesday 'in relation to certain alleged transactions involving that company.' Treacy, he said, had asked NIB to provide evidence that the sale of CMI insurance-based products had been properly authorised in Ireland.

The main reason the two journalists had gone to the Dáil to listen to the adjournment debate was to get a first-hand impression of the attitude of the finance minister to the story they had uncovered. This was their first opportunity to form such an impression because McCreevy had refused to comment publicly on the matter during the previous five days.

However, all of the information the minister had come out with so far was old hat. The fallout from the RTE revelations had been the dominant news story throughout the country since the weekend. Everybody knew about the involvement of the Revenue Commissioners and the Central Bank. The potential importance of the issue of proper authorisation for the CMI product had also been extensively reported.

Lee looked over at Bird, who was sitting beside him high above the minister in the Dáil press gallery. Boredom was beginning to register on the older reporter's face. Both had expected a much more lively parliamentary exchange than the one which was taking place below them.

The fact that one could count on two hands the number of TDs present in the chamber added to their growing disappointment. Lee looked back towards the minister who, by this stage, was going on about the investigative powers of the Revenue Commissioners and of the Central Bank.

It wasn't until the very end of his speech that McCreevy threw in something new – an insight, perhaps, into his own attitude to what had gone on at NIB.

'Under the provisions of the Criminal Justice Act, 1994, the (Central) Bank is obliged to report to the Gardaí, a suspicion that any entity it supervises has committed or is committing the offence of money laundering. Money laundering in this context embraces tax evasion.'

The minister then added: 'Let me repeat again in the strongest possible terms my complete intolerance of those who engage in tax evasion and of those who assist or abet tax evaders.' With this comment, the minister had delivered the last word in the adjournment debate.

The two journalists left the Dáil and headed to the basement bar in the new exclusive Merrion Hotel, across the road from the Department of Finance.

'That was a bit of damp squib,' commented Bird. 'I expected a much more heated debate.'

'So did I, but I thought the last thing McCreevy said was quite strong,' said Lee.

'What was that bit again?' asked Bird as the barman pulled two pints of Guinness.

'His comment about money laundering. To the ordinary person in the street, that probably sounds a little more sinister than tax evasion.'

'Maybe it does, but do you know what I thought was the most amazing thing about that adjournment debate?'

'What?'

'The fact that it was hardly a debate at all.' Bird was becoming animated now. 'The consequences of what we uncovered last week should have got the politicians much more excited. Did you see how few were in the chamber. They just didn't seem to want to get into it.'

Lee mulled over the point Bird had just made. NIB had not taken issue with the details the journalists had broadcast about them in the past five days. Surely then, it was reasonable to have expected a more passionate parliamentary condemnation of the bank. However, the reporter did appreciate that opposition politicians had found it difficult to get Dáil debating time allocated to the NIB issue.

* * *

The reporters only had to wait until the following day, Thursday, for serious criticism of National Irish Bank to begin in the Dáil. It came from the Labour Party spokesman on finance, Derek McDowell. The Labour TD had been allotted time to debate the Ansbacher accounts and the finances of former Taoiseach, Charles Haughey. Instead however, he used his time to have a swipe at the NIB offshore investment scheme.

McDowell started with an attack on the investors who used NIB's offshore facility for tax evasion.

'There are aspects of the NIB operation which are even more disturbing than the detail currently known to us in respect of Ansbacher.' McDowell had told his parliamentary colleagues. 'We are talking about the local businessman, the local hotelier, the local garage owner: people involved in cash businesses who ultimately couldn't resist the temptation to hide their earnings from the Revenue. These are not just a few people living in exclusive mansions. They are the middle classes, the respectable businessmen from all over Ireland ... I believe this is profoundly important and has the capacity to provoke a public reaction, public resentment way beyond Ansbacher.'

However, the Labour Party finance spokesman reserved his harshest criticisms for the bank itself.

'We know this scheme was devised and operated nationally. We know that a small number of people located in Dublin were dispatched around the country to talk to prospective clients and to sell them the product. We know that, in at least some cases, it was the bank or its reps who took the initiative of approaching individuals who they thought might be interested. This wasn't confined to any one branch. The clients were dispersed throughout the country .... This was a "head office exercise" and it is inconceivable that it could have been set up without the active complicity of senior management.

'The purpose of the scheme is also clear,' McDowell added. 'This was a way of laundering money, of hiding money. It may be that some of the clients had good or legal reasons to hide money, but the overwhelming likelihood is that these people were looking to avoid tax and the bank knew that.

'That one of the biggest banks in the State would be actively involved in touting a product, the primary purpose of which was to assist in the evasion of tax, is bad enough in itself but it also provokes more questions.'

The Labour Party spokesman ended by calling for the Central Bank Governor, the Chairman of the Revenue Commissioners, and the Secretary General of the Department of Finance to be summoned before a special Dáil committee to answer questions in relation to the way they police the banking system.

Neither Bird nor Lee were in the Dáil to hear the Labour Party attack National Irish Bank. Instead they were continuing to search for more information and clarifications about the offshore scheme. The bank had not yet issued a detailed commentary regarding the story broadcast the previous Friday. The fact that NIB had stayed quiet for so long suggested to them that the bank was finding it difficult to rebut the contents of their report. It also suggested that management at the bank were plotting a damage limitation strategy. It was the prospect of being on the receiving end of such a strategy which had spurred the journalists to continue digging for more information.

* * *

National Irish Bank finally issued its first detailed public statement about its offshore investment scheme at 6.10 that Thursday evening, 29 January. This was 24 hours after the adjournment debate in the Dáil.

Both Bird and Lee were pleasantly surprised when the NIB statement arrived. To their eyes it confirmed almost all aspects of the story they had broadcast the previous Friday.

This latest NIB statement spectacularly contradicted the letter sent to RTE by the bank's solicitors just two days before the story broke. The original letter implied that CMI alone had been responsible for the circuitous flow of money which saw the CMI funds re-deposited at the bank. In its new statement, however, National Irish Bank was finally admitting that it encouraged its customers to appoint NIB as their investment adviser. The bank was also admitting that it encouraged its customers to put their money back on deposit in their local NIB branch. The bank was effectively owning up to a previous misinformation campaign. This caused the journalists to wonder whether they should trust all the information in this latest statement.

> CMI policies offer investors the facility to nominate investment advisors in relation to the funds invested under their policy. Policy holders introduced by NIB generally nominated NIB as their investment advisor, a practice encouraged by NIB to secure an ongoing relationship with both the customer and CMI .... When making introductions to CMI, NIB encouraged those customers seeking an £IR denominated bank deposit investment to direct CMI to put the policy funds on deposit with NIB.

The issue of how easy it had been for customers to get at their money, once invested in the scheme, appeared to be clouded. At one point in the statement, the bank claimed that investors were not entitled to direct access to their funds. At another stage it was claimed that part of the reason for ensuring customer funds were re-lodged in NIB was to make it accessible for encashment purposes. The bank also went on to admit that shortcomings were identified in the administration of the scheme in 1994 and that as a result all the deposits were moved to a central location.

While the bank had confirmed a large part of what had been broadcast, it was claiming there was no evidence that NIB had knowingly colluded with tax evaders. The bank was also saying there was no evidence it had engaged in a campaign to identify customers for the purposes of tax evasion. This was a denial which did not impress the journalists as they read and re-read the statement.

'I think we should be quite careful when contacting our sources from now on,' said Lee. 'This statement looks as if it is aimed at frightening them off. It says the bank will vigorously pursue our material and our sources. Strong stuff, isn't it?'

'It sure is,' said Bird. 'But look at this bit.' The reporter was pointing to the last sentence at the bottom of the first page of the statement. 'The bank has a duty of confidentiality towards its customers and will vigorously pursue legal avenues to recover this stolen material and to bring to account all parties associated with the theft. The resources of its parent are being utilised in this respect.'

'The impression is that they will devote a huge amount of money to finding our sources.' Lee flicked through to the last page. 'Did you see here how they boasted that National Australia Bank was one of the world's largest banking groups.'

What neither of the journalists knew at that time, however, was that National Irish Bank had ensured that every deputy in the Dáil received a personal copy of its four-page statement. In addition, the bank had employed the services of professional lobbyists. These were given the job of briefing politicians about the bank's point of view.

The fourth-largest bank in the country was peddling the idea that NIB itself was a victim. Its argument was that RTE had selectively presented allegations about its offshore scheme. The bank was claiming that some disaffected party had stolen confidential documentation about a minor investment scheme. They told politicians that this disaffected party had maliciously used an intermediary to give the information he had stolen to the journalists. Now that it had been exposed, National Irish Bank's main defence was that the amount of funds involved in its offshore scheme was tiny compared to its total deposits. It was a defence that would be repeated by finance minister, Charlie McCreevy, in Tallaght the next morning.

* * *

Shortly after the NIB statement arrived in the newsroom, Bird and Lee learned that a new letter had been sent by the bank's solicitors to RTE.

This time the bank was threatening to get a court injunction to prevent the reporters publishing or using any confidential information they had. The solicitors were also demanding the return of all confidential bank documentation in the reporters' 'possession, power, or procurement'.

The letter from Matheson Ormsby Prentice bore similar hallmarks to the detailed public statement just issued by the bank. 'There can be no doubt that RTE, its servants or agents were aware that the receipt of such information occurred in circumstances of breach of confidence. We have already written to the Director of News of RTE in relation to this confidential information but have received no response .... Publication of confidential information will cause irreparable loss and damage to the bank and its customers.'

Apart from the threat of a court injunction, the solicitor's letter contained a very explicit warning. The bank wanted specific written undertakings from RTE, by noon on Friday, not to publish or use information about the bank. If these undertakings were not forthcoming Matheson Ormsby Prentice had been instructed to 'seek damages, including exemplary damages, for any breach of confidentiality, which you or your servants may commit, together with the costs of such proceedings.'

Fortunately for the journalists, both Ed Mulhall and Eamon Kennedy were fully aware of what they knew and could prove. As the RTE executives were contemplating their response to the latest legal threat from NIB, the Chief Executive of the bank, Grahame Savage, was preparing to swear an affidavit which would encapsulate his bank's version of the story.

> RTE's journalists have obtained confidential information about the bank and its customers .... They could use this information to engage in uninformed speculation which would be defamatory and damaging ... They ought to have known the information was released to them through a breach of confidence ... RTE has a list of bank customers who acquired CMI products ... RTE chose to publish reports which are defamatory of NIB .... The ill-informed nature of the reports carried on RTE and emulated in other sections of the media is defamatory and damaging to NIB and the interests of its customers .... The essence of the claim being made by RTE is that NIB have knowingly been involved in tax evasion by their customers, and have intentionally acted to facilitate such tax evasion .... It is not and never has been the policy of NIB to act in such a manner ... NIB does not wish to restrain RTE's fair comment on matters of public importance but are gravely concerned RTE ... will continue to damage NIB ... in a manner which is unconnected with any legitimate reporting role being played by RTE .... Irreparable damage ... RTE propose issuing further stories which involve the release of further confidential information...

Behind the scenes the professional lobbyists employed by the bank were dishing out all these comments, and many more, to anyone who would listen to them.

* * *

Lee and his cameraman exchanged troubled glances. It was Friday morning, a week after the CMI story was broadcast. The Revenue Commissioners' Press Officer, Vivienne Dempsey, was ushering them towards the foyer of the new Revenue office in Tallaght. She was trying to locate a suitable position for the pair to film an interview with Cathal MacDomhnaill, the Chairman of the Revenue Commissioners. However, it was neither the activities of the highly efficient Revenue press officer, nor the prospect of speaking with MacDomhnaill which had provoked the troubled glances. It was the comments finance minister, Charlie McCreevy, had just made to Lee which had the reporter and the cameraman stunned.

'What about here? Do you think this spot will do?' asked Dempsey as she brought the pair to a halt in front of the new Revenue reception counter.

'I'll leave it up to him,' said Lee gesturing to the cameraman. 'He's the expert on interview locations.'

'Yeah, it's alright,' said the cameraman, 'we can put him standing here, and if I shoot from this angle, we'll be able to get some of the office in the background.'

'Great so, I'll go and get the Chairman. I'll be back in a minute.' Dempsey disappeared into the crowd of Revenue employees and media people who had attended the opening ceremony.

'I've never seen McCreevy so testy,' confided the cameraman. 'You really got him annoyed.'

'I couldn't believe it,' whispered Lee. 'He must have got out on the wrong side of the bed this morning. All I did was ask a few questions.'

'He certainly didn't want to attack NIB,' added the cameraman.

'That's what threw me,' said Lee. 'I expected him to be bursting to have a go at the bank, especially after their statement last night effectively confirmed the whole story.'

'Yeah.'

'That's not all. That stuff he was saying about putting a perspective on the scheme, that was straight out of the NIB statement from last night.'

'He didn't like your questions one bit. Ridiculous and outlandish allegations, weren't they his words?' said the cameraman.

Vivienne returned with the Revenue Chairman in tow.

'Here we are then, where do you want him to stand?'

'Just here,' said the cameraman pointing to a spot he had chosen in front of the new Revenue reception area.

Lee's interview with the Revenue Commissioner Chairman was short but effective. MacDomhnaill said his officers were treating the NIB offshore scheme very seriously and had begun an investigation. He added that they were interested in more than just the avoidance of deposit interest retention tax. They would also be seeking to establish where the investors originally acquired the funds they put into the scheme. It was important to ensure that all income and other taxes due on these funds had been paid. The Chairman said, however, that the

Revenue investigation into the matter would take some time. The correspondent could see instantly that some of these comments would make it onto the *9.00 News* that evening.

On his way back to the RTE newsroom, Lee listened back to what the finance minister had said. He had recorded the interview using his own dictaphone while the RTE camera was rolling. But the more the reporter listened to his dictaphone tape, the more perplexed he became.

'These things must be borne in context,' said the minister on the tape, 'the total amount or revenue collected every year from all tax sources is of the order of fourteen billion pounds, or there about. The vast majority of taxpayers are compliant and pay their taxes on time – including business people – and the sums which you are talking about, there are a small proportion of the overall total sums of money involved in banks, and this should be borne in mind. And we must also bear in mind, and accept the reality of the situation, non-resident bank accounts are a very important feature of the Irish banking system. Considerable amounts of monies are held in Irish bank accounts by non-residents. The vast bulk of those people are genuine non-residents, but that is the same in all European countries as well. And secondly may I say, the question of tax evasion is not a unique Irish problem, nor is the question of residents having offshore bank accounts for tax evasion a unique Irish thing as well. So these things should be borne in mind rather than people going off half-cocked and making some ridiculous and outlandish allegations both against the Revenue Commissioners and against other people as well. These things will be investigated professionally by the bodies concerned and if any wrongdoing is about, it will be unearthed and appropriate penalties applied.'

'But Minister,' it was Lee's own voice on the tape now, 'are you trying to trivialise the suggestion that there was large-scale tax evasion involving so many people ... and are you trivialising the story as such in National Irish Bank?'

'I'm not,' replied McCreevy, 'but I'm trying to bring some reality to the situation with some of the outlandish accusations that have been made all round.'

'Like what? What kind of outlandish accusations?' it was Lee again.

The minister's retort was rapid: 'National Irish Bank have pointed out themselves that the sums of money involved represent nought point one per cent of their own total resources and that has put something in context.'

The minister went on to say that although tax evasion was a form of stealing, the State's revenue collection services have improved dramatically. But he didn't leave it at that.

'All I'm saying for people to do,' he went on, 'is to keep a sense of proportion about this, and I think it is important to do that in the light of some of the extraordinary scare-mongering that has gone on about tax evasion matters.'

Lee had pushed him three times in succession to say whether or not he would like to see the investors prosecuted if they had been involved in tax evasion. On each occasion, the minister refused to give a direct answer. All he would say was that it was a matter for the Revenue Commissioners to consider.

'Do you think the media is getting too hyped up about this National Irish Bank story?' the reporter had asked.

'At different stages, different ideas and problems come to the forefront of public attention, but I'm just trying to keep things in context,' replied the finance minister. 'Nobody condones tax evasion. As I said earlier in this interview is that it is a form of stealing. What I am trying to do is to keep things in perspective.'

By the time Lee got back to Donnybrook the reporter had listened back to his interview with McCreevy three times and he was still at a loss to explain the attitude the minister had displayed.

McCreevy had always been a pleasant enough individual when it came to his dealings with the media. Yet he had certainly not been in an affable humour today.

At about 1.40 that afternoon the finance minister listened closely to the radio in his ministerial car. The *News at One* programme was about to broadcast some of his interview about National Irish Bank. His press officer, Mandy Johnston, was at his side and in the days to come she would tell Lee that her minister was delighted with the three-minute clip of his interview which was broadcast that lunchtime. She would add that McCreevy was in jocular humour and felt he had had a very good morning. It would be a description of events which would compound the RTE reporter's confusion over how the Minister for Finance could have apparently changed his attitude towards National Irish Bank so quickly.

It had been less than two days since McCreevy had likened what went on at National Irish Bank to criminal money laundering. Suddenly he was using very assertive tones to tell the journalist that: 'National Irish Bank have pointed out themselves that the sums of money involved represent nought point one per cent of their own total resources... keep a sense of proportion ... keep things in context ... keep things in perspective ... will be investigated professionally by the bodies concerned ...'

When Charlie McCreevy spoke of 'ridiculous and outlandish allegations' earlier that morning, Lee had instantly feared the finance minister was becoming sympathetic to the bank.

* * *

Nevertheless, the NIB view of the world continued to make little impact in RTE. While McCreevy was being interviewed in Tallaght, RTE's solicitor, Eamon Kennedy, was drafting a letter to Matheson Ormsby Prentice. He was responding to the legal threats issued by National Irish Bank the evening before. In his letter, Kennedy wrote that the controversy surrounding the bank was of public interest and importance. He said the national broadcasting organisation was statutorily obliged to investigate and report on it. In addition he wrote: 'RTE is satisfied that National Irish Bank has no good grounds for instituting proceedings and therefore will resist any application for injunctive relief your client may seek in the High Court.'

At about 5.00 that Friday evening, however, lawyers for National Irish Bank walked into court. There they applied to Mr Justice Patrick Smith for an *ex parte* injunction to prevent the journalists from using the confidential information they had obtained.

Richard Nesbitt, Senior Counsel for National Irish Bank, read the affidavit of Chief Executive, Grahame Savage, into the court record. He also read out some of the correspondence which had passed between NIB and RTE.

The national broadcaster had been given just 20 minutes notice of the time and venue for this application. As a result, RTE was not represented in court and the judge granted the injunction. The effect was that Bird and Lee were prevented from using any documentation or information they had about National Irish Bank. They could make no use 'whatsoever' of any information identifying or tending to identify any customer account, transaction, investment or business done by any client of National Irish Bank.

Mr Justice Smith stipulated that the injunction should last for only ten days at which time the issues would be fully thrashed out in court.

With delays and appeals, however, it would take 50 days before the injunction was finally lifted. National Irish Bank's damage limitation strategy was succeeding. The RTE journalists had been well and truly gagged.

The Injunction Begins
to Bite

9.00 A.M., MONDAY, 2 FEBRUARY 1998

Bird and Lee considered the implications of the gagging order at a meeting in Ed Mulhall's office. Eamon Kennedy was also present. Ensuring the injunction was lifted had become their number one priority.

Mulhall was determined to demonstrate that muzzling RTE was a waste of time. He wanted his two journalists to find ways of continuing to highlight what had gone on at the bank. However, he insisted that in doing so they should respect the terms of the court order.

So far, neither Bird nor Lee had given the bank any opportunity for personal attacks. Since they wanted to keep it that way, they would have to be extremely careful while the injunction was in place. Meanwhile, they would all have to start working on an affidavit capable of convincing a judge to lift the order.

They looked closely at the specific wording of the page that came from the court. It read:

30th January 1998

National Irish Bank Limited
& National Irish Bank Financial Services Limited
v
Radio Telefis Eireann

Judge Patrick Smith granted the following injunction:

'An Injunction restraining RTE by itself, its servants or agents or otherwise howsoever from making use whatsoever (and in particular from making any publication of) information falling within the categories described in the following Schedule.

SCHEDULE

1. Any documentation or information identifying or tending to identify a customer of the plaintiffs
2. Any information or documentation identifying or tending to identify an account of a customer held with the plaintiffs

3. Any information or documentation identifying or tending to identify the transaction on any account of any customer held with the plaintiffs

4. Any information identifying or tending to identify investments made by or business transacted by any customer of the plaintiffs

The terms of the injunction appeared more restrictive than the journalists had expected. Mr Justice Smith had specifically ordered RTE to make no use 'howsoever' or 'whatsoever' of information likely to identify any NIB customers. Rigidly interpreted, this implied the reporters could not contact any client of the bank. To do so would, by definition, involve the use of information identifying a customer, a technical breach of the injunction.

When he granted the injunction Mr Justice Smith had indicated that his order need not be too strictly interpreted. Yet the journalists were fearful that if they continued to contact bank customers, NIB would run back to court to lodge complaints against them. The more the bank complained the more difficult it would become to get the injunction lifted.

In addition, any NIB protestations to court would become media events. Such occasions would afford the bank an opportunity to discredit the two reporters and their work.

National Irish Bank was putting about the story that it had been defamed by RTE. This was clear from the sworn affidavit of Grahame Savage which had been read out in court. Yet more than a week after the story was broadcast, the bank had given no indication of how it had been defamed. No substantive challenge to what the journalists reported had been raised. The bank had not even asserted that any aspect of their broadcast was either untrue or inaccurate. Also notable was the fact that NIB had not instituted any legal proceedings for defamation against RTE.

The fact was that there were no grounds to support the multi-million pound defamation action which NIB desperately wanted to file. This, however, was cold comfort to the two journalists. Both were fearful that inactivity on their part could open the way for the bank's propagandists to launch an offensive.

The professional lobbyists employed by NIB were busy at work in political and media circles. With the injunction in place, it would be easier to convey the bank's version of events. If the bank were unchallenged in the corridors of power, then the image of the national broadcaster and its reporters could be damaged.

For Bird and Lee the best protection from such forces was to continue investigating their story. The bank could be kept on the defensive only as long as the two journalists kept coming up with new information. If they were barred from contacting bank customers, however, they would find it very difficult to make headway and the bank's spin doctors would gain the upper hand.

The most obvious thing about the gagging order was that RTE was the only media organisation affected by it. Newspapers and other broadcasting stations had been left to investigate freely.

On any other occasion, RTE would have been outraged to have been singled out for such restraint. In the current circumstances, however, there was a positive side.

As long as journalists in other media outlets continued to investigate the offshore scheme, there was some hope the bank and its spin doctors would be kept on the defensive.

The weekend newspapers had carried quite a few articles regarding the fallout from the RTE revelations. Two reports in particular had caught the attention of the journalists, their boss and their solicitor.

One of the reports had been written by Richard Curran, the Business Editor of the *Sunday Tribune*. The second was published under the by-line of John McManus, the Irish political correspondent for *The Sunday Times*. Both of these newspaper reporters had uncovered pieces of information which could add to RTE's chances of winning in court.

In his *Sunday Tribune* article, Curran said he had come across an individual who had been seeking to invest a large sum of money offshore in 1995. NIB had recommended that this individual sign up for the CMI personal portfolio. The bank sent the individual an application form. Attached to the application form was a one-page letter detailing the advantages of the offshore scheme.

Curran wrote in his article that the one-page letter from the bank 'seems to spell out in no uncertain terms that if a person wanted to hide their funds for whatever reason, it would be easy to do so.' The *Sunday Tribune* article went on to list some of the selling points NIB employed to hook the investors.

In his article in *The Sunday Times* John McManus had taken a different angle. The headline across the top of his report was, 'Bank knew customers were tax evaders.' He was quoting 'authoritative bank sources' and 'senior management sources'.

According to his report these people had told *The Sunday Times* that 'managers openly discussed how the scheme could be used to dodge tax.' This was contrary to what Grahame Savage had sworn in his affidavit the previous week.

The Chief Executive of the bank had sworn that NIB had not knowingly been involved in tax evasion by its customers. The fact that his statement was now contradicted by senior managers unknown to RTE would be useful in drawing up RTE's response.

However, the most useful element of *The Sunday Times* article was a quote it carried from a senior NIB source: 'It is not true to claim, as RTE has done, that we operated (the CMI scheme) as a tax evasion scheme. What did happen was that some managers were acutely aware that they had customers who were a little hot and this allowed them to get the money off their books and bring it back clean.'

Such a comment from a senior NIB source was devastating for the bank. It suggested that NIB executives did, at times, operate the scheme to help some of the bank's customers launder hot money. In its public statement the previous Friday, NIB had insisted its executives had not colluded with customers in evading tax. The bank also denied that executives tried to identify specific customers for the purpose of tax evasion.

Revenue laws dating from 1982 make it clear that aiding and abetting a person to evade tax is a criminal offence. If caught, an individual faces a fine of £1,000 and/or one year in prison for each offence under summary conviction. If the case goes before a jury the penalty rises to £10,000 and/or five years in prison for every person assisted.

With such penalties on the statute books, surely no bank would put in writing that it was colluding with tax evaders. The risks of self-incrimination would be too big.

Bird and Lee had always suspected it might be impossible to find definitive documentary evidence of NIB knowingly colluding with tax evaders. However, the McManus article had given them an idea. If a banker was willing to be interviewed by *The Sunday Times* and offered the quote they had just read then surely RTE could get a similar insider to testify about how the offshore scheme operated.

The RTE reporters had, after all, spent the past three weeks in secret discussions with NIB insiders. If their faces could be hidden and their voices disguised then perhaps one of the bankers could be convinced to give a television interview.

The testimony of an NIB insider on national television would surely keep the bank's spin doctors on the defensive, while RTE's lawyers worked at getting the injunction lifted.

The reporters noted that the terms of the court order did not prevent them from approaching current or former employees of the bank. Nor did the injunction prevent them from reporting what newspaper journalists had uncovered.

By the time Bird and Lee left Ed Mulhall's office that Monday morning they had a very clear strategy in mind. The national broadcaster has a statutory obligation to report on important issues of public interest. The newsroom team was determined to show National Irish Bank that RTE takes its obligations very seriously.

* * *

Monday is normally a quiet day at the offices of any Sunday newspaper. The *Tribune* was no exception. However, Lee's luck was in. Richard Curran was one of the few journalists manning the *Tribune's* office when he phoned that afternoon. Lee was delighted to have found him so easily, and so willing.

The *Tribune's* Business Editor was unfazed by the presence of the television camera. He simply stood in his editor's office, looked Lee in the eye, and rattled off the advantages of the offshore scheme. He was quoting the one-page letter NIB sent to the prospective investor which he had described in his report on Sunday.

'No customer name on any account ... no probate required in case of death ... tax free ... easy accessibility of the funds ... and exact same deposit account and interest rate as client already had.'

Curran's delivery was direct and effective, exactly what the television reporter had hoped. The list of advantages matched everything RTE had learned about the scheme.

What was different now, however, was that the *Sunday Tribune* reporter had seen documentary evidence of the way the personal portfolio product had been marketed.

The letter Curran spoke about could possibly prove that NIB openly peddled the scheme to Irish investors as a way of changing a named deposit account into an easily accessible tax-free numbered account with no probate requirements. In its last big public statement, and in its sworn affidavit, the bank had claimed that no such evidence existed. If Lee could get his hands on the letter Curran had seen, it would help RTE's chances in court.

The television reporter and his cameraman stayed a good deal longer than expected in the *Sunday Tribune* offices that afternoon. Like all good journalists, the *Tribune's* Business Editor would not reveal his source. Nevertheless, he did prove enormously helpful.

Discussions were held and phone calls were made. By the time Lee arrived back into the RTE newsroom shortly after 5.00 that evening he had a copy of the letter, referred to by the *Sunday Tribune*, safely in his hands.

Before he could consider the letter properly, however, RTE's economics expert rushed off to an edit suite. There he crafted a news report using interview clips from both Richard Curran and John McManus of *The Sunday Times*.

If NIB bosses were watching either *Six One* or the *9.00 News* that Monday evening they should have received a clear message. It would take more than a court injunction to stop RTE covering this story.

* * *

Lawyers for RTE considered applying to have the NIB injunction discharged in advance of the High Court hearing scheduled for 9 February. It was decided, however, that such an approach might backfire. An affidavit outlining the RTE case still had to be sworn. A rushed affidavit could result in the presentation of an incomplete and ill-thought-out case.

NIB had received RTE's list of questions on 20 January but Grahame Savage's affidavit had not been filed until ten days later. This delay had given the bank's lawyers lots of time to do their homework. RTE's lawyers would have to do the same. They confessed there was a high risk they would lose the case.

The core argument for NIB was that confidentiality was attached to banking information. RTE's case would be that there is no right to such confidence where illegality has occurred.

In similar cases in the past, the courts always ruled in favour of the confidentiality argument. The rationale usually offered by judges was that there is no way to compensate for a breach of confidence. Defamation, if it occurs, can be nearly always remedied by monetary compensation. Confidence, however, once breached and lost, can never be restored.

The NIB injunction had not been based on a fear that further television reports could defame the bank. If it had been, then a judge would probably see that RTE had enough money to compensate the bank for the damage it might inflict. Consequently, most would deem that no 'irreparable' damage could then result. In such a situation many might lift the injunction.

However, NIB had cleverly centred its application around the issue of confidentiality. Its legal argument was that no amount of money from RTE could ever remedy a wrongful breach of confidence. From the point of view of the judiciary, the balance of convenience in such situations tended to favour the continuation of the injunction.

This was why RTE's lawyers were so concerned about their chances in court. It was also why they believed it would be foolish to rush into court before 9 February.

Neither Bird nor Lee could hide their disappointment when they heard how pessimistic their legal advisers were. As far as the reporters were concerned, the scheme they had uncovered was crooked. The possibility that it could be made illegal for them to investigate such a scheme disturbed them.

They had two days before the RTE affidavit would have to be sworn. The strongest possible legal case had to be presented. More facts and more evidence were required.

* * *

Lee began a painstaking re-examination of all the documents and notes collected so far. He re-read the internal memos, the solicitors' letters, and the bank's public statements. There was nothing new in any of them.

He picked up the one-page marketing letter, acquired after his trip to the *Tribune*. The business card of an NIB investment manager named in an earlier memo, was stapled to it.

The advantages listed on the page had been aired on television the day before. However, the disadvantages of the scheme had been overlooked. Only two disadvantages had been listed on the page. Lee read down through the sheet of paper twice. Then he called Bird over to his desk.

'I think I've just twigged something that might help us,' he said.

'What is it?' asked Bird.

'NIB's case is that everything we have unearthed resulted from administrative shortcomings in its investment division and not illegal activities on its part. Our affidavit has to destroy this argument.'

'That's right.'

'Well look at this,' said Lee pointing to the first disadvantage listed on the sheet.

'What about it?'

'It shows the investors had to pay a total of nine per cent of their initial capital to invest in the scheme. One per cent was paid up front. Then another one point six per cent was deducted each year for five years.'

'So it was very expensive. We knew that already.' Bird was wondering what Lee was getting at.

'But we didn't know it was exactly nine per cent.'

Lee held up the internal bank memo referring to the businessman from Cork who left the scheme after five months.

'These memos, Charlie, make it clear that this nine per cent charge was unavoidable. Every investor had to pay it whether they were in for five weeks, five months, or five years.'

He switched to the internal letter from the branch manager in Mullingar.

'This letter to Boner points out that NIB's sales team fully explained the charges to investors before they signed them up.'

Lee then returned to the marketing letter. He pointed to the third advantage, listed as, 'Cautious Investment'.

'This letter,' he said, 'plainly boasts that, once offshore, the investor's money can be rapidly transferred back to NIB.'

'So what's your point?' Bird said. 'There's nothing new in that.'

'Just think about it, Charlie. The bank openly asked wealthy depositors to fork out nine per cent of their savings. For this they offered them the privilege of earning the exact same interest rate they were already earning and the exact same account they already had.'

'And the name on the account would be replaced by a number,' added Bird.

'Yes. And what's more, we know from its statement last Thursday that NIB actively encouraged its customers to choose this investment option. But why would anyone recommend such a lousy option to a client if they did not at least suspect the client was a tax evader?'

Lee paused to let the point he had just made sink in. Then he added, 'NIB insists there is no proof it did anything wrong. But if we put all our bits together like this, surely we have prima facie documentary evidence that the bank was engaged in illegality. This has to improve our chances in court.'

Belfield Bridge

The driver of the blue Toyota Starlet pulled into the side of the Clontarf Road. He switched on the hazard warning lights and turned off the engine. Then he checked his wing mirror, opened his door, and walked calmly to the rear of the car. There he fumbled with his key-ring for a few seconds before he found the right key. He always had to think about which key to use to open the boot of his wife's car.

The little Toyota had been running low on petrol and he had told his wife he would fill it up on his way into town. His added justification for borrowing it, he had told her, was that it would be easier to park. His own car was larger, and would be awkward in the city centre on a Friday afternoon.

Fortunately, his wife kept the boot of her car relatively tidy. He pulled back the worn floor covering to reveal the spare wheel. He lifted it out and placed it upright, leaning it against the bumper of the car. Then he stood looking up and down the road for about 30 seconds to see if he recognised anyone. When he saw the coast was clear, the driver leaned forward into the boot and withdrew a white plastic bag from the bottom of the spare wheel compartment.

He rummaged through the bag for a few minutes before taking out some sheets of paper. He looked at them, smiled, and put them to one side. Carefully, he folded the plastic bag and placed it back exactly where he had found it. Next he picked up the spare wheel, clipped it into position and re-fixed the floor covering. He then took the pages in his hand, shut down the boot, and got back into the car. Twenty seconds later, the blue Toyota was back in the middle of a stream of traffic trundling down the Clontarf Road, heading for the city centre.

It was shortly after three in the afternoon when the Toyota pulled into a parking spot just 50 yards from Busáras, the main bus station in the middle of Dublin. The driver locked the car, put a coin in the parking meter, and checked for familiar faces. When he saw none, he crossed the road and walked briskly towards the station.

Busáras was crowded with people waiting to leave the city early for the weekend. Arrival and departure information cackled continuously out of tinny speakers set into the ceiling. The driver brushed past the passengers and headed straight towards the snack bar at the far left-hand corner of the station.

When he got as far as Gate 16, the departure gate nearest to the snack bar, he stopped and looked around for one last time. Nobody was taking any notice. He then walked on past the snack bar, and came to a halt at a sign which said, 'Luggage: Open 8.00 a.m. to 7.45 p.m.; Bags £2 per day, Rucksacks £3 per day'. The driver took out his wallet and withdrew a small blue ticket. He handed it to the middle-aged attendant who disappeared into the store room. When he reappeared one minute later, the attendant was carrying a light-brown duffle bag which he handed over the counter. Three minutes later the banker climbed back into his wife's car. There he opened the duffle bag, took out a file, and inserted the pages he had removed earlier.

* * *

Bird looked up at the sky and resigned himself to the fact that he was going to get soaked. He had been deep in thought when he left the newsroom and it was not until he reached the Stillorgan Road that he remembered his overcoat. The reporter had been instructed to wait outside the entrance to University College Dublin at Belfield Bridge, the only flyover on the Stillorgan dual carriageway. The bridge was only half a mile from the RTE studios so it made sense for him to walk. The temperature was unusually warm for early February and Bird would have managed without his overcoat if it had not started to rain.

The reporter stood beside the 30 mile an hour speed limit sign and waited as arranged. It was a 3.45 in the afternoon and thick black clouds ensured the light was fading rapidly.

A bus shelter was positioned only 25 yards from where the journalist was standing. He did consider dashing into it for protection as the rain began to pour. He was afraid, however, that if he did, his contact could miss him and drive off. That was too big a chance to take considering the week he had just had. Bird decided that getting soaked to the skin was preferable to missing this particular rendezvous.

The reporter had spent most of the week, along with Lee, Mulhall and Eamon Kennedy, preparing legal arguments for court. It was hard work. They had been holed up indoors, in the company of solicitors and barristers, until the previous evening. Then, shortly after their affidavit was finalised and signed by Mulhall, they learned the injunction hearing had been postponed for a further two and a half weeks. This had annoyed himself and Lee, both of whom were hoping the legal constraints which had been imposed would be lifted much sooner. They had learned the hard way just how much of a hindrance the court order could be.

Now, as the rain pelted down on Belfield bridge, Bird peered in at every motorist who drove up the slip road into the university. He had no idea what type of car to expect but he certainly knew which face. Despite poor visibility, many of the drivers appeared to recognise him. Five or six flashed their lights in salute. Bird felt particularly conspicuous standing alone in the rain on a flyover bridge, just 25 yards from a bus shelter.

The reporter looked down at the puddles now beginning to form at his feet and wondered how long more he would have to stand there. When he looked back up he saw the flashing lights of a Toyota Starlet which had slowed to a stop at the opposite side of the junction. The reporter instantly recognised the face of the duffle-bag banker sitting behind the steering wheel. Bird scurried across the road, pulled the passenger door open, and jumped in.

'Horrible weather,' said the banker. 'I hope you weren't waiting too long.'

'About ten minutes. I got here just as the rain started. Came out without my coat but, sure, I'll dry out quick enough.' Bird wiped the rain from his face.

'I'll just drive into the university,' said the banker as he pulled away from the kerb and switched on his left indicator. 'They have a few big car parks in here.'

'That's fine,' said Bird as he clicked his seat belt into position.

Two minutes later, the banker manoeuvred his wife's car into a space at the far end of the university's No. 1 car park. He switched off the engine and unhooked his seat belt. Then he swivelled around, reached into the back seat, and picked up the bulging folder from underneath his brown duffle bag. As the banker lifted his folder into the front of the car Bird's heart began to thump.

When he had phoned the banker the previous day, the reporter wanted to ask him about doing a television interview. It would be a difficult request. He would need time to explain how the insider's voice and face could be disguised. Such an interview would be risky for the banker so it was best not to discuss it over the phone. That was why Bird had suggested today's meeting, although once again, it had been the NIB insider who chose the location.

The banker had told Bird over the telephone that he had information about 'something bigger than the offshore scheme'. However, he said his new material could not be used until the furore caused by the previous story died down. Bird had decided not to push him too hard about what he had meant. He figured it was unlikely that a bigger story about NIB could possibly land in his lap.

Two weeks had passed since the first offshore investment story had been broadcast. In that time, lots of people had phoned Lee and himself with tales supposedly more scandalous than the NIB scheme. But they had all fallen short of expectations. When the duffle-bag banker suggested he too had an even bigger story, Bird was curious about what it could be. Yet, he didn't really expect a lot. How could the same bank be involved in a second hooky scheme?

Now though, the banker felt safe. The fading daylight, the steamed up car windows, and the southside car park, all afforded him a degree of camouflage. It was as good a time as any to give the reporter an insight into how NIB had run its business.

'I have something I think you should see,' he said to the wet reporter.

Bird said nothing in reply but his eyes were glued to the bulging black folder which the driver still held in his hands. He watched as the banker took a single sheet of paper out of his folder and handed it to him. 'Take a look at this. It's a letter from an NIB branch manager in 1993. I think it speaks for itself. It will give you some idea of the type of things that went on.'

Bird took the one-page letter in his hands and examined it carefully in the fading light. The first thing he noted was that it was short and handwritten in blue biro. The second thing was that it was on NIB headed note paper. The third, and by far the most striking, was the term 'Hot money potential' clearly visible towards the end of the page. The reporter gasped when he saw these words. He decided to read the letter properly.

It came from the National Irish Bank branch in Church Square, Monaghan and was dated 5 April 1993, barely a month before the government announced the tax amnesty. It was addressed to another manager, whose surname and address were not included on the handwritten letter. The correspondence read as follows:

> During interview today with good customer at this office (gives name of his customer) he advised me it may be worth your while contacting below named: (includes the name and address of a farmer, from Munster) Milks 250 cows. 'Hot money potential'. Let me know how you get on.

National Irish ✦ Bank

A member of
National Australia Bank Group

Church Square
Monaghan
Tel (047) 81862, 81337
Fax No. (047) 82872

Date 5/4/93

[Manager's name and branch]

During interview today with good customer at this office

[Customer's name and address] *he advised me it may be worth your while contacting below named:*

[Name and address]

Milks 250 Cows
" Hot Money potential "

Let me know how you get on

The bank had repeatedly asserted that it had never been focused on colluding with customers in evading tax. It also continued to claim there was no evidence of a campaign to identify specific types of customers for the purpose of tax evasion. This letter did not mention the offshore investment scheme and contained nothing to indicate that the Munster-based farmer was subsequently invited into the scheme. There was nothing either to indicate what the recipient of the letter did once he learned of the milk farmer's 'potential'. There was no obvious direct link between this correspondence and the offshore investment scheme. As a result, the letter on its own would not be enough to prove collusion with tax evaders. Nor would it be enough to prove a campaign to identify customers for tax evasion purposes. However, there was no doubt it could undermine the credibility of NIB's denials and in the current circumstances, that had to be good for Bird and Lee.

Bird discussed the letter with the banker for about ten minutes before his curiosity finally got the better of him.

'That's a pretty big file you have there,' he said, nodding towards the bulging folder on the banker's lap. 'Is that all about NIB?'

'It is,' replied the banker, tapping the black file with his fingers. 'There's enough material in here to wipe out the bank.'

'You mean there are more stories to be told, apart from the CMI scam?'

'There certainly are. That CMI business is only small beer compared to some of the other stuff that went on,' replied the banker.

'Like what?' asked Bird, excitement written all over his face.

'I have to be careful about this material. I can't let you use it for a while.'

'Don't worry,' replied the reporter, 'I promise I won't do anything without your agreement.'

The banker took one look at the earnest expression on Bird's face and caved in.

'Okay,' he said. 'Just to give you some idea of the kind of things I mean, you can have a read of this.'

The NIB insider opened his folder and pulled out three pages which had been stapled together. He handed them to Bird. The prospect of glimpsing more of the material the banker carried around in his duffle bag had the reporter completely enthralled.

'This is an extract from an internal audit report for the NIB branch in Carrick-on-Shannon,' said the banker. 'The full report is much longer than this but these few pages are really all you need.'

Bird looked down at the first of the three pages he held in his hand. It included a list of the NIB executives to whom the report was circulated. It also included the names of the people responsible for its preparation. The NIB banker stayed very quiet while Bird scanned through the second page. Rain continued to pelt onto the roof and windscreen of the Toyota as the reporter flicked over to the third page. He could hardly believe what he saw. The comments on this page related to an examination of overdraft interest charged on a small sample of customer accounts.

The very first paragraph consisted of only one sentence. Yet it was a sentence that Bird would remember for a very long time. It said 'Interest charges were increased without legitimate reason or customers' knowledge on twenty accounts in November 1989 and thirty-three accounts in February 1990.'

The reporter read the entire page three times before lifting his head to look at the banker.

'This can't be for real,' he said. 'It has to be a hoax.'

'Oh, it's for real, all right,' the banker replied. 'It went on all the time.'

'But how could any bank put something like this in writing about one of its own branches?'

'Well they did, and not just for that branch. It was widespread.'

Bird was stuck for a reply. He watched as the banker delved back into his folder and plucked out another bunch of pages.

'Here's another one,' he said. This time he handed Bird seven pages from an internal audit report for the Carndonagh branch of NIB in Donegal. The date on this report was August 1990.

Charlie flicked through the pages, faster this time. He stopped as he came to the one which summarised what the auditors found when they examined a small sample of customer current accounts. Again he stared in disbelief at the first paragraph. It read, 'interest charges were increased without legitimate reason or customer knowledge on 12 occasions in May 1990 and 13 occasions in February 1990. This practice also applied in 1989.'

The NIB insider watched as the stunned reporter flicked back to the first page and began reading the Carndonagh report for a second time. As soon as he saw that Bird was finished, the banker gathered his reports and put them back in his file.

'There are plenty more where they came from,' he said.

'Really?'

'Yeah, but I have to careful with them.'

'Okay,' replied Bird. 'But tell me one thing. When the auditors discovered the illegitimate charges, what did the bank do?'

'Not a lot,' replied the banker.

'Was the money paid back?'

'No.'

'Were the managers disciplined?'

'No.'

'Were the customers ever told?'

'No.'

'Good God!' was all the reporter could say. The banker had been right all along. He did have material for a much bigger story than the offshore investment scheme.

It took Bird another five minutes to convince the banker to allow him to bring the audit reports back to RTE to show George Lee. He also persuaded him to part with another letter which seemed to prove that the practice of illegitimate interest charging also went on at another NIB branch in Dublin. The reporter waited until he had all these documents, and the hot money letter, safely in his hands before returning to the subject of the offshore investment scheme.

The banker listened carefully as Bird outlined the reporting strategy Lee and he had settled on. Bird explained that they were looking for an NIB insider to do a television interview with the aid of face and voice distortions.

'I'll give it some thought,' the banker said when Bird asked him out straight to consider being interviewed. 'I'll think about it over the weekend and let you know early next week.'

It was a 5.15 when the small blue car slowed to a halt outside the main entrance to RTE. Bird grabbed the new documents to his chest, opened the door, and said his goodbyes. The banker watched through the rain as the journalist disappeared in the direction of the television building. He then drove off towards the toll bridge which would bring him back home to the northside of town.

* * *

Lee had spent Friday morning in the town of Dundalk where the Minister for Social, Community, and Family Affairs, Dermot Ahern, has his constituency office. Official monthly unemployment figures had been published showing another drop in the jobless total. A continuation of a well-established downward trend in Irish unemployment. Lee decided to cover it because the trip to Dundalk would provide a mental break after four weeks on the NIB trail.

The success of the bank in applying for the injunction had hardened his determination to stick with the banking story. The effect of the gagging order, and the knowledge that the bank's spin doctors were working against himself and Bird, left him with little option but to investigate further. It would take a while longer before issues like unemployment, and interviews with the social welfare minister, would return to the top of his reporting agenda.

As he drove back towards Dublin in the mid-afternoon, Lee wondered how Bird would get on with the duffle-bag banker. He had taken four phone calls from his colleague on the way to Dundalk but had heard nothing since just before lunch. The economics reporter was still disappointed that the injunction hearing had been postponed. An interview with a banker, however, would be some consolation. He believed it was unlikely that either himself or Bird would learn anything new from an interview. They had, after all, grilled many insiders about the offshore scheme and knew what they all had to say. But it could be electrifying to put a banker on television to tell the nation that the shocking facts they had reported were true.

Lee arrived back in the newsroom just as it started to rain. Ten minutes earlier he would have seen Bird walking up the Stillorgan Road in the direction of UCD. He checked through his taped interview with Dermot Ahern and wrote a short television script. Thirty-five minutes later he dropped his completed unemployment report into the news output room. Then he hauled Ed Mulhall out of his office and the two of them went off to the canteen for coffee. That was where they were when Bird burst in.

'You'll never believe what just happened!' announced the reporter, obviously excited.

'He said he would do the interview?' suggested Lee trying to guess why his rather damp looking colleague was so charged up.

'No, that's not it. But he said he would think about it,' replied Bird.

'So what is it?'

'It's bigger than the CMI, and no judge will dare stop us this time.'

'Stop us doing what?' Both Lee and Mulhall asked this question at the same time.

'This!' said Bird plonking his new documents onto the table. 'Wait till you read through these. It's all on the third page, the rest hardly matters.'

Lee picked up the internal audit report for Carrick-on-Shannon, dated April 1990. Without hesitation, he followed Bird's instructions and flipped to the third of the three stapled pages. There was a number, nine, at the bottom of the page, so he knew immediately this was only a small extract from the audit report.

BRANCH: CARRICK-ON-SHANNON

REPORT POINT: Interest on Current Accounts

WEAKNESS/POTENTIAL ADVERSE CONSEQUENCE

It was noted that Interest Charges were increased without legitimate reason or customers' knowledge on twenty accounts in November 1989 and thirty-three accounts in February 1990.

The above practice could lead to loss to the Bank through customer dispute, litigation or adverse publicity.

REMEDIAL ACTION REQUIRED

Interest amendments may only be made to correct Branch errors. The practice of "loading" interest in this manner must be discontinued.

RESPONSE BY BRANCH MANAGEMENT

We note that as and from now only branch errors can be corrected using interest amendment sheets.

While we only loaded interest rates for customers who were very demanding, we were certain that we were safe in applying the additional interest charges. No queries ever came back from customers who interest was loaded.

We note and confirm that this practice will be discontinued.

9.

The word 'Revenue' at the top of the page indicated that it referred to the internal auditors' findings in relation to the revenue raised at the Carrick-on-Shannon branch during the period in question. The top right hand corner of the page carried the words 'Core 2' and immediately under it 'Report point 1'. This signified that branch revenue was the second of the core areas examined by the auditors, and that the comments to follow referred to the first point about branch revenue the auditors wanted to discuss.

Two lines later the precise nature of the 'report point' was detailed as 'Interest on Current Accounts'. The next paragraph, was headed 'Weakness/potential Adverse Consequence'. This was the paragraph which had stunned Bird when he read through it first. Now it was having the same effect on Lee.

He read it out loud. 'It was noted that interest charges were increased without legitimate reason or customer knowledge .... The above practice could lead to loss to the bank through customer dispute, litigation or adverse publicity.' He stopped to check that Mulhall, who was now sitting at his side, was still reading along with him. Then he carried on, reading to himself.

The next heading on the page was 'Remedial Action Required'. Under this heading was written: 'The practice of "loading" interest in this manner must be discontinued.' There followed a section on the page detailing the 'Response by Branch Management' to the recommendations of the internal auditors. It read: 'While we only loaded interest rates for customers who were very demanding, we were certain that we were safe in applying the additional interest charges. No queries ever came back from customers whose interest was loaded.'

Lee looked over at Bird who, at this stage, had a cup of coffee in his hands and a grin all over his face.

'It says here, Charlie, that the practice will be discontinued. Do you know if that was what happened?' he asked.

'I imagine it did, but I really don't know,' replied Bird.

'Do you know if NIB ever paid back the money?'

'I was told that it didn't. They kept it quiet and there was no disciplinary action.'

'So who knew about it?' asked Lee before flicking back to the first page of the report and seeing the answer for himself.

The circulation list for this audit report included Mr Jim Lacey, the Chief Executive of the bank at the time; Mr Frank Brennan, the General Manager; Mr Kevin Curran, the Regional Manager for the Carrick-on-Shannon area; Mr Hilary Flood, Head of Credit Bureau at NIB, and Mr John O'Reilly, Manager at NIB's Carrick-on-Shannon branch. Obviously all of these executives knew of the illegitimate interest loading on unsuspecting customers. Others who clearly knew included the executives involved in the particular internal audits. They, however, had acquitted themselves with a recommendation that the practice must be 'discontinued'. However, Lee wondered if the Chief Executive, the General Manager, the Regional Manager or any of the others ever made any attempts to pay the money back to the customers.

Lee and Mulhall finished reading the extracts from the Carrick-on-Shannon report. They then moved on to the second document Bird had left on the table. It consisted of seven pages copied from the internal audit report for the NIB Branch at Carndonagh, and dated August 1990. The cover, the circulation list, the table of contents, and a summary of the audit findings had all been included. In addition, there was a summary of audit points, and a profile of the Carndonagh branch. The last page in the bunch was titled 'Revenue' and contained a discussion of current account interest. It was almost a carbon copy of the 'Revenue' page they had seen for the Carrick-on-Shannon branch.

Under the heading 'Weakness/Potential Adverse Consequence,' it read: 'interest charges were increased without legitimate reason or customer knowledge, on twelve occasions in May 1990 and thirteen occasions in February 1990. This practice also applied in 1989.... This could lead to loss to the bank through customer dispute, litigation, or adverse publicity, due to the issuance of an Interest Certificate for the correct amount, or a customer's accountant querying why an amended statement was issued at interest charging periods.'

The 'Remedial Action required' section recommended: 'The practice of "loading" interest must be discontinued.'

The 'Response by Branch Management' was even more interesting than it had been for Carrick-on-Shannon. The manager of the Carndonagh office stated: 'The practice of loading was initiated for accounts that were either constantly in excess of their agreed limits (as evidenced by appearance in the Morning Report), or were the subject of frequent urgent S/L reports. Through discussion at branch the implications of loading were highlighted, but for obvious reasons immediate cessation was not feasible. The practice has been gradually scaled down and will be totally eliminated before the next charging period.'

The last two sentences of the branch management response were illuminating. They suggested the reason the interest loading could not be stopped too quickly was because customers would notice. Queries and awkward explanations would probably result. It would also mean the branch would have to pay back the money, something it obviously had no intention of doing.

In August 1990, the Carndonagh branch of National Irish Bank was staffed by five permanent and two temporary employees. The manager,

Mr JM Mullen, had been appointed to the branch in June 1989, fourteen months before the internal examination. Mullen was authorised to give out loans of up to £10,000 without security or collateral. When security was provided he could go as high as £40,000. At the time the internal audit was performed, the branch had a total of 138 outstanding loans, valued at £322,000. It had also made provisions of £51,000 for bad debts. Carndonagh's contribution to NIB group profits had grown from £70,000 in the second half of 1986 to £169,000 in 1989. All of these details had been included in the branch profile compiled by the internal auditors.

Apart from its practice of secretly loading interest onto unsuspecting customers, the Carndonagh branch was also pulled up for its control over 'cash holdings levels' and 'foreign draft order forms,' both of which the auditors said were weak.

The circulation list for the Carndonagh report was similar in pattern to the list for Carrick-on-Shannon. Jim Lacey, Frank Brennan and Hilary Flood were all included. The Regional Manager on the circulation list this time, however, was Dermot Boner who was subsequently promoted to Head of Retail Banking at NIB. Mullen, the branch manager at Carndonagh, was also named on the list.

All of these people knew interest was illegitimately levied onto customer accounts. It was obvious again, however, that none of them had made much of an effort to see that the money was repaid.

When Lee and Mulhall had finished reading the Carndonagh report they moved without comment to the next item Bird had brought back. It was a short letter written by Brian A. Earl, Deputy Manager of the NIB branch at Walkinstown in Dublin. Earl's letter, addressed to Mr KJ Martin, Senior Manager, Credit, had been written on 11 July 1990. It was a response to a different letter sent by Martin to Earl the previous day concerning the issue of 'Interest Charged on Accounts Current'. Earl's response consisted of just one sentence:

'We hereby confirm that the practice of interest loading on customer accounts without any prior agreement or notice to the customer will cease immediately.'

Lee looked over at Bird. 'It looks like this interest-loading was practised in quite a few places.'

'Yeah. He said it was widespread,' replied Bird, referring back to what the banker had told him in Belfield. 'He said Cork was particularly bad.'

'Did he give you any reports for Cork?' asked Lee.

'Not yet, but he has a thick black folder, and he said there was more where these came from.'

'What about Walkinstown? Does he know how long the loading went on there before this letter was written?'

'No, we never got to discuss that.'

Lee and Mulhall then looked at the final letter Bird had brought back.

'Milks 250 cows. "Hot money potential". Let me know how you get on.'

They read through the letter twice. The three of them looked at each other and said nothing. Twenty-four hours previously they had wallowed in disappointment after learning that their court hearing had been postponed. Now everything had been transformed. The offshore investment scheme was still very important, and lifting the injunction would remain the priority. But if Bird and Lee maintained their composure and continued to work as a team, they believed this NIB scandal was destined to become an even bigger news story.

The Quest for the Interview

MONDAY, 16 FEBRUARY 1998

If the drive up to his house had not been so impressive few would have thought he could be a millionaire. He didn't look remotely like a businessman. He stood in his stockinged feet as he answered the door. A large, rumpled, middle-aged man. He wore a loose, open-necked shirt and creased cotton trousers. Bird and Lee could tell he was nervous about the consequences of letting them into his County Cork home. A long and bitter dispute with National Irish Bank had undermined his financial security. This may have contributed to the aura of vulnerability he gave off as he greeted the RTE pair.

He led the two journalists into a large, expensively furnished lounge with an impressive view of the surrounding countryside. The businessman knew well why the journalists had travelled from Dublin to see him. Bird had phoned him earlier in the day after hearing from a source that this businessman had been invited into the offshore scheme but had decided against it. The businessman had been receptive on the telephone. He said he was willing to meet the reporters. Yet, as he eased into his chair and stretched out his stockinged feet, he began to behave like a man who was having second thoughts.

The reporters explained they were particularly interested in learning how National Irish Bank had marketed its offshore investment scheme. They assured him they knew he had not invested in the scheme. The reason they travelled so far, they told him, was to see if he would explain the details of how NIB approached him. Any examples of the marketing literature or letters he received could be very useful. In addition, they were interested to know exactly why he decided against the scheme.

The businessman spoke with a Cork accent. He discussed his grown-up family and his health. He spoke at length about a bad experience he had with a newspaper journalist in the past. A file full of press cuttings relating to his experience was produced. The more he spoke about his newspaper episode the more cagey he became about speaking out freely.

Bird eventually became bored listening to complaints about journalists. He had travelled to Cork to hear about NIB, not about some seven-year-old gripe.

'Look, I don't mean to be rude,' Bird interrupted, 'but we don't have too long. Could we just talk about National Irish Bank?'

'A right shower of bastards,' replied the businessman in a contemptuous tone.

'Bastards?' said Bird, happy now he had made his interruption.

'That's what they are in my book,' replied the Corkman. 'They've tied up my money and it's ruining my business.'

'But your money isn't in the offshore scheme.'

'Offshore scheme?' scoffed the man from Cork. 'Offshore scam would be more like it.'

'But you're not in it, isn't that right?'

'I wouldn't touch it with a barge pole.'

'So what happened when they approached you?' asked Bird.

'I told them no. I saw right through it. It was just a rip-off and that's what I told them.'

'How much did they want you to put in?' asked Bird.

'I only had ten thousand pounds,' replied the Corkman, in a quieter voice.

Lee didn't believe what he was hearing. He had sat quietly taking in everything the businessman had said about his family, his health, and about journalists. Obviously the Corkonian had plenty of worries, and for that he felt sympathy. But Lee had seen the application form and brochure for the CMI product. Both made it clear that the minimum investment allowed was £50,000.

'You must have had more than ten thousand,' said Lee. 'Wasn't fifty thousand the minimum?'

'Fifty thousand! I'd never have that kind of money.'

The journalists exchanged glances. They knew the businessman was holding back. His line of business involved very large sums of money and the house they were sitting in was nothing short of a mansion. One of the bank insiders had told them the dispute between the businessman and the bank arose over a very large amount of money. There was no way they could believe NIB had asked this man to pay almost £1,000 in fees to put another £9,000 into the same bank account he already had.

'But why would they try to rope you in, if you only had ten thousand pounds?' asked Lee.

'Well I had a bit more money in England, I had eight thousand there, so I could have put in a total of eighteen thousand.'

'And that's all?' asked Lee.

'Yes that's all.'

From the very start of their investigations Bird and Lee had tried to be scrupulously careful about the things people told them. All information had to be checked and rechecked or else backed up with documentation. Yet they had to accept that a few of the people who gave information had private agendas of their own. A businessman in bitter dispute with NIB over several hundred thousand pounds was quite likely to fall into this category. The threat of television exposure might encourage the bank to agree to whatever settlement terms he was looking for. If this was what the businessman wanted then his invitation to Bird and Lee to travel to his house in Cork could have been primarily motivated by a desire to help himself, rather than a desire to help their journalistic investigations. The fact that he was not prepared to tell the truth about his dealings with the bank suggested to the reporters that their trip to Cork may have been a waste of time. Investigative journalism is difficult enough when a source refuses to trust the journalists. It is far more difficult, however, when the journalists cannot trust the source. Bird wasn't having any of it. It was time to get tough.

'I don't believe you,' he said.

'What do you mean?' asked the businessman in his strong accent.

'You must have had more money than that,' replied Bird.

'As God is my witness,' protested the businessman, 'that was all the money I had.'

The conversation about the money then went around in circles until Bird got fed up.

'Okay,' he said, 'let's forget about the amount of money. What we really want is for you to do a television interview for us.'

The businessman was startled.

'An interview? About what?'

'About the way the bank's executives approached you, the tactics they used, the things they said, and so on.'

'I don't like the sound of that.'

'But we can disguise your voice, and your face. We'll make sure that nobody will recognise you,' replied Bird.

'No, I'm not going to do that.'

'Okay so,' said Bird. 'There's no point in us wasting any more of your time. We better get going. It's a long way back to Dublin.'

Bird's abruptness unsettled the businessman. He didn't seem to like the prospect of the journalists he had invited to his home leaving so soon. As Bird and Lee got up to go he offered them whiskey and tried to engage them in some more conversation, anything to delay the departure. The journalists, however, figured they could have stayed all night and still be unsure about what the cute Corkman was telling them.

Bird went into the hall as if to leave while Lee stayed in the room gathering his notes. But the businessman still wanted to talk.

'I wrote a letter to Argus,' he said.

'Don Argus?' asked Lee taking it all in again. Don Argus was the Chief Executive of NIB's parent group, National Australia Bank. He had also been a Director of NIB since November 1990.

'Yeah, Don Argus. I wrote to him nine months ago.'

'Why did you write to him?'

'I wanted to tell him about my problems with the bank. I told him the CMI scheme was a scandal.'

'Have you got a copy of the letter?'

'Come on, George, let's go,' shouted Bird from the hall.

'I'm coming now, Charlie,' replied Lee although he had no intention of moving until he got more information. Bird's interruption, however, seemed to spur the businessman on.

'I have the letter in my office, but my solicitor has the key so I can't get it at the moment,' replied the businessman.

'What did you say in the letter?'

'I offered to fly him over to Ireland and put him up in a hotel so I could tell him about what was going on at the bank,' claimed the businessman.

Out in the hall, Bird could hear that progress was finally being made. However, he stayed where he was, fearful he might put the businessman off if he re-entered the room. Every now and then though he would shout in, as if he was fed up waiting. Every time he did so, the businessman confessed more information to Lee.

It took another ten minutes before Lee and the businessman joined Bird in the hall. By that stage the businessman was happier and much more relaxed. He may have started off with his own private agenda and a distrust of journalists, but he had warmed to the younger reporter. He confided that he had money in several non-resident accounts and one day received a phone call from his NIB branch. The manager arranged to come and see him at his work place. An NIB investment sales person and one of the bank's Dublin-based investment managers, arrived with him.

They brought a range of charts and reports, and delivered a lengthy presentation. They pushed him hard to sign up for the scheme but the businessman balked as soon as they mentioned the charges. He said he couldn't believe it was so expensive and yet offered no interest rate advantage over the accounts he already had.

Some time later, a firm which owed the Corkman a lot of money went into liquidation. NIB immediately froze all his bank accounts including some he claimed had been set up in false names. This action by the bank denied the businessman access to the cash-flow he required to keep trading. An amount in excess of £600,000 was involved. If NIB would not loosen its grip, then the businessman could soon become bankrupt. This had been the source of his bitter dispute with the Australian-owned bank. It was also the main reason he had written to Don Argus. His letter incorporated all his complaints about the way NIB was treating him, including his disgust at the attempt to rope him into the offshore scheme. The fact that nine months had passed since his letter was written, but that no resolution had been found to his dispute, explained much about his demeanour. He had enough problems to deal with already without compounding his stress by going on television.

The journalists would have left without any of this information if they had not resorted to the 'good cop/bad cop' routine they employed. Bird's abruptness, combined with his threat to leave early, came as a shock to the Corkman who then responded to Lee's more sympathetic and patient approach. When the time came for the reporters to finally leave, the businessman was in a happier mood. Perhaps he was relieved he had shared all his problems, or maybe he was happy that the reporters would continue to investigate. But whatever the reason, he seemed genuinely sorry to see them go. He offered them both a bottle of whiskey to take back to Dublin but they refused. Lee took out a business card and wrote Bird's number on the back of it. He gave it to the businessman before they drove off.

Later that night, as they sat at a bar, the two reporters chuckled about the antics of the businessman whenever Bird had shouted in from the hall. Pushing him for an interview about how the offshore scheme was marketed would be a waste of time. NIB would attack his credibility because of the bitterness engendered by his long-running dispute.

But while the two reporters were musing over the events of the day, the businessman sat alone in his lounge and enjoyed a quiet laugh of his own. He had a business card to prove the reporters had called. The thought of the worry he would cause NIB with tales of the visiting journalists now gave him some pleasure. In the days and weeks to come the Corkman would take to phoning NIB headquarters at odd hours. He always asked for the General Manager, Frank Brennan, knowing he would not be there. Every time he was asked if he would like to leave a message, he would say, 'yes, just tell him Charlie Bird phoned'. Imagining the irritation such a phone message would cause to the bank gave the Corkman some kind of thrill.

* * *

The RTE reporters knew exactly where their investigation was heading. The internal audit reports for the NIB branches at Carrick-on-Shannon and Carndonagh had signalled the way. They also knew, however, that if they were going to accuse NIB of stealing from its customers they would have to start from scratch with the same journalistic approach they had taken to the offshore investment scheme. Every new fact would have to be corroborated. Interviews would have to be sought. The legalities of reporting about the situation would have to be examined. There was no point taking on such work while the story of the offshore scheme still needed attention. In addition, the reporters felt certain that no other journalists had access to the documents they had. As a result, they were unlikely to be beaten to the second leg of their story by any newspaper.

Both Bird and Lee were happy to do nothing with the audit reports for the moment. This was precisely what the duffle-bag banker had asked them to do. Most of their efforts would continue to be devoted to rebutting NIB's insistence that it did not knowingly invite tax evaders into the offshore scheme. The pending court hearing over the injunction meant they still needed evidence, or some testimony, to challenge the NIB claim. The trip to Cork had been an effort to secure such an interview but it didn't pay off. The reporters were still on the lookout for a banker who would testify.

Lee had begun to notice some odd clicking sounds when he was using his home telephone. Perhaps such noises had always been present on his phone line but he had just not noticed them before. He was now very keenly aware that himself and Bird were in possession of information which could do enormous damage to the fourth-largest bank in the country. He was also aware that the bank had promised to spend a lot of money to discover which insiders were passing on information. Lee convinced himself that these factors had made him super-sensitive to the sounds on his phone line and that the few clicks he heard were nothing to worry about.

Nevertheless, he was becoming increasingly reluctant to engage in detailed telephone conversations with Bird about either their sources or their information. Crossed telephone lines were quite common. It would be disastrous to have someone inadvertently, or even deliberately, tuning in to their top secret investigations. Shortly after the trip to Cork, he discussed his telephone concerns with Bird. They both decided to stick to their GSM mobile phones as much as possible. All the experts said GSM technology made mobile phones impossible to tap.

It was Lee's mobile phone number that Bird dialled as soon as he heard the good news late on Tuesday night. The duffle-bag banker had made contact. He had agreed to be interviewed about the offshore investment scheme the following day. He laid down no conditions, except that his identity be disguised and protected. The reporters were delighted. They discussed the type of information the interview should focus on and where it might take place.

Neither reporter could recall a bank insider spilling the beans in similar circumstances in the past. This would be a big breakthrough. If all went well, they could offer the interview to *Prime Time*, RTE's current affairs flagship programme. Senior executives at the station had indicated that *Prime Time* was interested in any further significant developments relating to National Irish Bank.

* * *

Just before lunch on Wednesday 11 February, RTE cameraman Robin Boyd arrived at the hotel. He booked in alone and collected the key to his room. It was a busy hotel, located outside Dublin. Boyd spent some time shifting the furniture about in his room, and finding the best position for his camera. He wanted a background neutral enough to ensure the location would not be easily identified. When he was satisfied, the cameraman went off and had lunch. Bird arrived just after 2.00 p.m.

The staff at the hotel recognised the face of the television reporter. Yet nobody said anything as the two men went off to the room. They waited there for another half hour before the banker arrived. He came without his duffle bag and did not seem perturbed by the presence of the camera. He willingly put on Bird's jacket to aid his disguise. Then he settled into the chair Boyd had positioned for the interview. Bird checked that the banker was comfortable and then launched into his questions. He asked him what the customers were told about the offshore investment scheme.

The banker spoke carefully and seemed to consider his answers before he delivered them. He said, 'customers were informed that the bank was concerned that the Revenue Commissioners may have access to bank records at a future date, and that the bank could not guarantee the customer total anonymity from the Revenue Commissioners. They were told that this scheme would remove their names completely from the account, replace the name with a number, and on that basis it would guarantee them protection from Revenue inspection of the bank records, should that arise at a future date.'

Bird asked the banker if it was his 'understanding' that a substantial number of the people invited to join the scheme 'had sensitive monies, undeclared monies, or basically hidden money.'

'That is correct,' said the banker. 'That is my understanding from my knowledge of the scheme.'

'So what type of people were they?' asked Bird. 'What type of money had they got?'

'The figures could vary, anything from fifty thousand pounds up to hundreds of thousands of pounds,' replied the banker.

'Did the bank know who they were targeting?'

'The bank was well aware of who they were targeting,' said the insider without hesitation.

'I want to be absolutely clear of this,' said Bird, 'this was money that was undeclared, money that the Revenue Commissioners knew nothing about. Is that correct?'

'That is correct,' replied the banker. 'The product was specifically aimed at those types of people.'

'Do you believe that the senior management in the bank knew what they were marketing and who it was being marketed to?' asked Bird.

The banker replied, 'it would be highly unusual for any type of product within National Irish Bank to be launched without the sanction of people at the highest level.'

The banker went on to explain that an expensive offshore investment scheme where the money was lodged back into an Irish bank account offered no advantage to people with legitimate savings.

He also commented on the fact that it was launched around the same time as the government announced an amnesty for tax evaders to come clean. He said that many investors were concerned that if they declared for the tax amnesty they might be subjected to closer scrutiny by the Revenue Commissioners in the following years.

The interview lasted about half an hour but it was punctuated by several interruptions. The banker insisted that he would only talk about knowledge he had personally gleaned from first-hand experience. When he had no direct experience relevant to a question, he refused to give any answer. On each occasion when this occurred, the banker would stop the interview to explain to Bird why he could not answer.

At all stages the duffle-bag banker was cool, calm and deliberate. He gave the impression of being in complete control of his own actions and words. He had not been rushed, paid, or bullied into this interview by the reporter. He was participating because of a calculated and conscious decision he had taken himself. This banker had no intention of speculating, or of saying anything which he would not be able to stand over.

The findings of the internal branch audit reports which the NIB banker had delivered the previous Friday were never brought up during this interview.

As soon as the interview was over, the banker put his own jacket back on. He shook hands with Bird and Robin Boyd. Then he calmly left the hotel room on his own. Twenty minutes later, the RTE cameraman gave his key back to the hotel receptionist. She was a little surprised that the guest was checking out less than four hours after he had checked in.

* * *

Lee had spent most of the day at the Company Registration Office in Dublin's Parnell Square researching information about National Irish Bank. That was where he was when Bird phoned to say he was rushing back to RTE with the interview tape. He said all had gone well and that he believed the banker had delivered the comments they required. Bird had asked Lee to meet him at RTE when he got back so they could view the interview together.

Two hours later, the reporters commandeered the tape player in Ed Mulhall's office. They sat quietly and took notes while watching and listening to what the banker had said. The tape was compulsive viewing. The words of the banker had damned the NIB scheme. His face would have to be blocked out and his voice substituted with that of an actor. But this might serve to underline for television viewers just how serious his comments really were. It would also demonstrate that he took a great personal risk by giving the interview.

The banker had been strong in his assertion that the circuitous offshore scheme held no attraction for legitimate investors. He had stressed that the scheme had been deliberately targeted at accounts which had not been declared to the Revenue Commissioners. This, he said, was consistent with the way the scheme was marketed. It had been sold quietly. Typically, NIB would employ aggressive national and local advertising techniques to push financial products. This one, however, appeared to have been sold under the counter, to customers who fitted a certain description.

Lee thought about the banker's insistence that no legitimate saver could be bothered with the scheme. A few quick calculations confirmed the logic of what the banker had claimed. The tax regime had been the key to his assertion.

A special 10 per cent rate of DIRT tax had been introduced by the Government in the budget of 1993. This is the tax deducted at source from the interest earned on deposit accounts. The standard rate of DIRT tax at the time was 27 per cent. To avail of the special new 10 per cent rate, depositors had to make a declaration to the Revenue Commissioners. They would then receive an official stamped form from the tax office. This would certify that their savings account qualified for the low rate of tax. The interest earned on accounts which had not been declared was still liable to the 27 per cent rate of DIRT tax.

This tax system was clearly designed to penalise savers who refused to make a declaration to the Revenue Commissioners. As a result, they were the only ones who could possibly gain from the scheme.

Any married couple with £100,000 to invest could legitimately put their money on deposit in NIB for five years. The interest payable on the account could be, say, 10 per cent. One tenth of the legitimate interest earned would be taken each year for DIRT tax. At the end of the five years, the investors' deposit would have grown to £154,000 and there would be no remaining tax liability. This is significantly more than the savers would get if they opted for the NIB offshore scheme instead.

If they had invested £100,000 in the offshore scheme, they would lose £1,000 of their money on the first day. This would cover the one per cent 'up front' charge levied by CMI. The remaining £99,000 would then be channelled back into an NIB deposit account, yielding a 10 per cent return. Interest would begin to accumulate. But at the end of every year £1,600 would be deducted. This would cover the 'annual management charge,' quoted by NIB as '1.6 per cent per annum of the original capital invested'.

After five years of such charges, the amount in the deposit account would have grown to just £149,000. This is more than £4,000 below what would be achieved by a legitimate investment outside of the scheme. On top of this, the offshore investors would still be liable to pay five years' worth of DIRT tax as soon as their offshore investment matured. This would cost another £6,000. The result is that the legitimate investors in this case would lose out by a total of more than £10,000 if they invested in the NIB offshore scheme.

If, after a year or so, the investors needed to gain access to their money, for some emergency, then the disadvantage of the offshore scheme would be magnified. The entire costs for five years would be deducted before the money was returned. No such costs would accrue on an ordinary deposit account at their local NIB branch.

The logic of such mathematics strongly supported the banker's assertion. It seemed to make no sense for NIB to market this scheme to customers not interested in tax evasion. The fact was, however, that NIB had boldly admitted in its public statement that it actively encouraged its offshore investors to ensure their money was re-deposited at their local branch. Lee was convinced that NIB's assertion, that it did not target certain types of customers for the scheme, was beginning to look very flimsy indeed.

The reporter also worked through some further rough calculations. According to his estimates, NIB earned over a million pounds in commission for selling the CMI product to its own customers. He also calculated that CMI earned in excess of £3 million for investments it did not even have to manage. The figures also suggested that the Irish exchequer may have been diddled out of £26.5 million as a result of the scheme. This was enough to cut one per cent off the top rate of income tax on budget day.

Bird and Lee considered the implications of all these figures. They wondered if they might influence the finance minister's 'perspective' on the NIB scheme. They wondered also, if Charlie McCreevy would consider the interview with the NIB insider to be loaded with 'ridiculous and outlandish allegations,' the kind he had complained about in Tallaght. By the time they vacated Ed Mulhall's office, the two journalists had concluded they had the new material they needed to justify a big *Prime Time* report.

Prime Time

MONDAY, 23 FEBRUARY 1998

A lot of work still had to be done with the interview tape before it would be ready for transmission on the news. The reporters feared that if NIB knew what had been said, the bank would try to stop it being broadcast. All those involved in its preparation agreed to keep quiet about what it contained.

One of RTE's video editors was given the task of modifying the tape. Using high-tech equipment, he ensured the banker's face was replaced with a blur. An actor was called in to record a voice-over, matching the words of the banker. This was then edited on to the interview tape with the help of a sound engineer. Legal advice was taken regarding the safety of broadcasting the banker's remarks. Bird ordered new camera shots of the NIB headquarters and of the Baggot Street building which housed its financial services division.

A lot of other work was required for the *Prime Time* report. A television producer, Stephen Carson, was assigned to work on the project with Lee.

The culture faced by reporters in the News division of RTE is quite different from the culture of Television Current Affairs. News reporters and correspondents concentrate on short, accurate, factual, reports. They work alone with a cameraman and a video editor, turning stories around rapidly, and concentrating on the news value of the items they are dealing with. At all stages, they maintain total control over their own reports. The result is a tough and stressful job which both demands and promotes individual self-reliance, self-confidence, and independence.

Television Current Affairs reporters' work differs considerably from that of News reporters. They tend to concentrate on longer, more considered, thought-provoking reports, many of which have a type of campaigning quality. Theirs is also a tough and stressful job but they rarely, if ever, work alone. Professional television producers, trained in the art of programme making, generally have a big input into the way each story is filmed and told. Among other things, producers like to dictate camera angles, lighting, and the style of the reports.

Lee had been working in RTE for five and a half years. He had spent three of those years as an economics reporter in the Current Affairs division. As a result, he knew exactly what to expect when it was decided that he should be the one to prepare the NIB report for *Prime Time*. Bird, on the other hand, had been in RTE for almost 25 years. For the first seven he worked as a researcher, but for the last 18 years he had worked exclusively as a reporter in News. He was delighted when the Editor of Current Affairs, Noel Curran, and his Executive Producer, Eamon O'Connor, enthusiastically consented to devote *Prime Time* resources to the NIB story. However, it was not long before the clash of cultures between the two divisions undermined Bird's personal enthusiasm for the project.

Current Affairs had some big undertaking already in the pipeline by the time the News reporters approached them on Thursday, 12 February. The first opportunity *Prime Time* could offer for the screening of a lengthy report about NIB was the following Thursday, 19 February. This one-week delay would be long by News standards but was very short by Current Affairs programme-making standards. It would provide time for a producer to be freed up, for production facilities to be assigned, and for a considered report to be put together. Lee was looking forward to the task, but Bird was feeling impatient. If the newsroom had decided to go it alone, Bird's interview with the banker could have been broadcast on the Monday evening news. This would be well in advance of the *Prime Time* slot. However, RTE bosses had been promoting the idea of co-operation between News and Current Affairs. They had also made it clear that they wanted *Prime Time* brought in on the NIB story. Bird was a bit disappointed about the delay but, in the end, was happy enough to agree.

The following afternoon, the producers from *Prime Time* watched the video of the interview with the banker. They considered the implications of having to disguise his voice and identity. If the banker's face had to be blurred and his voice replaced with that of an actor, then the remaining visual contribution of the original interview would be minimal. To allow weakened visual images to be the centre piece of a lengthy TV report would invite viewers to switch off. These were the reasons why the *Prime Time* producers wanted to film a new actor, in silhouette, voicing the words of the banker. They also argued that this approach would be a better way to protect his identity than simply blurring the image of his face.

Having worked for so long in Current Affairs, Lee had little difficulty in accepting these arguments and believed the decision was correct. He understood the effect they were trying to achieve and how serious they were about the image of their programme. However, he dreaded the prospect of having to tell Bird.

The older reporter reacted badly when he was told about *Prime Time's* intentions. He was furious that they would not use his original interview. He protested that it had taken a lot of work to get the banker to agree to talk on the record. Risks had been taken, time had been spent, an actor had already been employed. Bird pointed out that the original interview tape had qualities that were impossible to replicate. It showed the dingy conditions in which the interview really took place. It showed the natural pauses that followed after each question was asked. It was real. Even with a blur on his face, Bird believed the banker would be seen as a person. He was not some shadowy silhouette on a wall. The original interview tape was good enough for News. Bird could not accept that it was not good enough for Current Affairs.

As the days wore on, Bird became increasingly sensitive over what he began to think of as interference by outsiders in a newsroom story. He complained that *Prime Time* had first dictated the date of the broadcast. Then they had dictated that a dramatised version of his original interview was required. Finally, he said he heard *Prime Time* producers speak about 'their' NIB story. This for him, was the last straw. As far as he saw it, the NIB story belonged to News, not to Current Affairs. Eighteen years of rivalry between the two RTE divisions had shaped his outlook. Four days after suggesting that Current Affairs should piggyback on his interview with the banker, Bird got mad. He told Lee he had decided not to let *Prime Time* use his interview after all.

Now it was Lee's turn to be furious. He had already put a lot of work into the *Prime Time* report. He knew it could have a big impact. Lee agreed that everything known about the offshore scheme, needed to be pulled together. This was the best way to ensure the bank was kept on the defensive. He explained that all financial stories are difficult to explain on television. In a lengthy report about an offshore scheme, the audience could easily get tired. He protested that viewers would not care about a silhouette on a wall, as long as the story was compelling. Lee insisted that the *Prime Time* producers were best placed to get the message across. They have skills which reporters do not have. They are experts at making visually appealing programmes. The producers had no intention of interfering with the content of the report. Their sole objective was to ensure that the story hit home.

Bird could not help how he felt about *Prime Time*, but he did not blame Lee for those feelings. Lee, on the other hand, did not see *Prime Time* as a problem. After a heated debate the two reporters calmed down and agreed they should concentrate on the bank. The culture of RTE News had clashed with the culture of Current Affairs. Fortunately, the tension that resulted did not last very long.

* * *

The following day Bird heard back from a source. An NIB executive with an insight into the scheme had been overheard talking. He had told colleagues that he personally had sold the CMI scheme to two Fine Gael politicians in one region of the country. Bird's enthusiasm was back.

The prospect of catching two legislators breaking the law excited the news journalist. However, the NIB executive had not named who his customers were. This made them difficult to catch. There was no way of knowing if the Fine Gaelers, reportedly involved, were TDs or local politicians. In addition, the indiscreet banker had not revealed the year in which he brought the politicians into the scheme. Without more information the search would be fruitless. Nevertheless, the sniff of skulduggery had perked Bird up. His concerns about *Prime Time* melted away.

* * *

At 6.00 on the evening of Wednesday, 18 February, Lee settled himself in front of a television in the newsroom's Oireachtas unit. He had broken away from preparing for *Prime Time* because Maurice O'Connell, the Central Bank Governor, was about to be quizzed by a parliamentary committee. The Oireachtas unit had a direct feed from Kildare House, the place where the governor was being questioned. This ensured the proceedings could be recorded for use later on. However, Lee wanted to see it all for himself. The governor was expected to speak about a broad range of issues. Interest rates, the exchange rate, Europe's single currency, and property prices. All these things, and more, were on the agenda. How the Central Bank supervises the activities of the high-street banks was also up for discussion and this was the topic which interested the reporter most.

So far, the governor had uttered no public comment relating to the RTE revelations about the National Irish Bank offshore scheme. A Central Bank team had been on the NIB premises investigating the revelations for almost a month. Surely the members of the 'Joint Oireachtas Committee on Finance and the Public Service' would ask the Governor for his views.

It was about eleven minutes past six when Maurice O'Connell settled into position opposite the row of TDs and senators who were on the committee. The prospect of being quizzed by a group of politicians held little apprehension for him. Long years of experience at senior levels in the civil service ensured that the governor knew how to be avoid being tripped up. Maurice O'Connell stayed in his chair for one hour and twenty minutes. Yet, the NIB story took up only five minutes of that time. The answer he gave when Fianna Fáil TD, Sean Flemming, asked him about NIB was typical of his approach.

'I don't want to talk about the details of the case, and certainly don't want to make any judgement about it until we have completed our investigation.' It was the kind of answer which would signal to the politicians that they would get nothing from the governor about National Irish Bank.

The Labour Party finance spokesman, Derek McDowell, tried a different approach. He wanted to know what it would take for the Central Bank to rescind NIB's banking licence.

'Am I right in assuming that if it was alleged that a bank was facilitating, or might be facilitating, tax evasion, that you would not regard it as your role to investigate that?' he asked the Central Bank Governor.

'No. It would be our duty to report it to the guards if we had reason to believe that one of our institutions was engaged in this activity,' came the reply.

'But you wouldn't investigate it as such?' pushed McDowell.

'No, we wouldn't investigate it. It would be a matter for the Gardaí.'

'You wouldn't see it as a reason to deny a banking licence, or to question the licence of a bank?' asked the Labour Party spokesman.

The governor thought for a second before giving his answer. 'I'm sure we would. Probably. Certainly we would look upon it as something where we would have to take some action.' Then he quickly added: 'That is, if it were proven.'

McDowell looked more satisfied now. He asked a follow-on question: 'To what extent does the Central Bank concern itself with the way in which a bank might be using its facilities, the products it might be offering, the sort of facilities it might be offering to customers, to clients? Or is it just concerned that it has its [financial] ratios right?'

O'Connell paused, and shifted in his seat, before answering this one. 'Our fundamental requirement has to be prudential. What we have to establish is that they are conducting their operations in an orderly fashion. If we became aware that they were colluding in tax evasion, as I said, we would report it to the guards.'

'But it is not one of those things you go out and look for?' McDowell knew the answer but the question was for the record.

'No, we don't look for it. No. That is not what we are about really,' replied the governor. 'I think I said earlier that we are not tax investigators.'

This exchange between the governor and the Labour Party spokesman only lasted a few minutes but Lee found it very worthwhile. The Central Bank boss had indicated that the licence of any bank found guilty of colluding with tax evaders would be questioned. Now there was a new relevance to NIB's dogged insistence that no evidence had been uncovered to substantiate any claim that it had colluded with tax evaders. If such evidence was uncovered, Maurice O'Connell had just told the politicians that NIB's right to continue banking in Ireland could possibly be withdrawn. For the Australian-owned bank the stakes could hardly be higher. The NIB statement that it would use 'the resources if its parent' to 'bring to account all parties' associated with passing information to Bird and Lee had not been frivolous. On the basis of the information available to the journalists, National Irish Bank was now in considerable trouble.

* * *

There was a lot of work to do the next day. Scripts for the news and current affairs reports had to be finished. Extra camera shots and graphics were required. RTE lawyers wanted to pore over the reports to ensure they were legally safe. Meetings of all sorts would have to take place. With so much to be done, Lee decided to travel to work earlier than usual. He wanted to beat the traffic.

Fifteen minutes after leaving home, Lee pulled into the RTE car park. He reversed into position, got out of his car, shut the door, and then double checked that it was locked. Two minutes later he walked through the newsroom doorway. Bird had arrived before him, equally eager to get started. They went off to the canteen together to plan out their day over a cup of coffee.

The reporters stuck rigidly to their tasks and the hours went by very quickly. By late afternoon, the three-and-a-half minute news report had passed all its checks and was ready for broadcast on the early evening news.

It began by reminding viewers how the offshore scheme worked and mentioned that four investigations into its operation were still going on. One investigation was being conducted by the Revenue Commissioners, another by the Central Bank. The findings of both of these would be kept secret. A further investigation was being conducted by auditors from National Australia Bank's European headquarters in Scotland. They were not obliged to publish their findings. The final investigation was being conducted by the Department of Enterprise and Employment. This was aimed at trying to establish if NIB had the necessary authorisation for the sale of the CMI scheme. The Department was still refusing to comment publicly on this matter, although NIB had admitted almost a month earlier that they had no such authorisation.

The remainder of the news report focused on NIB's insistence that there was no evidence that it knowingly helped people evade tax. The words of the duffle-bag banker were broadcast. He spoke about hot money, and about how the bank told customers the offshore scheme would guarantee them protection from the tax man. The news report also made reference to the fact that RTE had possession of a letter directing one bank manager to check into the 'hot money potential' of a farmer with 250 cows.

Bird, Lee and their boss, Ed Mulhall, were delighted when this report was transmitted high up in the first section of *Six One*. It could succeed in shifting public attention onto the role the bank played, away for a while from the names of the investors. The High Court hearing regarding the interim injunction was only one week away. It was the role of the bank, not the role of the investors, which would be the key to that hearing.

The *Prime Time* report was not completed until after 8.00 p.m. It was nine minutes in duration and contained many elements which had not been included in the news. The report mentioned the tax amnesty, described the way the offshore scheme worked, and incorporated a lot of the quotes from the banker. It highlighted how lucrative the scheme was for tax evaders, for NIB and for CMI. The big loss to the exchequer was outlined. Clips from the Charlie McCreevy interview in Tallaght were also incorporated. The finance minister's press woman had stressed how happy he was when he first heard his interview. The government's attitude to the scheme was part of the story so McCreevy's comments about the allegations being 'outlandish and outrageous' was relevant. Brian Bohan, the former President of Institute of Taxation, was also included in the *Prime Time* report. Bohan is a lawyer and a tax expert. He had been astonished some weeks earlier when the details of the scheme had been outlined to him by Lee. He highlighted the difficulties the NIB sales people might face if it were proven that they had knowingly assisted customers to evade tax. Another clip of McCreevy was used where the finance minister confirmed the seriousness of the offences highlighted by Bohan. The possibility that the Central Bank might question NIB's licence was mentioned. The report also showed pictures of Jim Lacey and Alex Spain. Lacey had been chief executive of NIB for the first half of the 1990s. Spain had been, and still was, chairman of the bank. The point was made that if these men did not know about the scheme, then they certainly should have known.

The soundbites of the banker all focused on the way the scheme was marketed, what it was suitable for, and how the customers were approached. The visual images and the graphics were strong. Although there was no doubt that some of the investors had broken the law, Lee's report unequivocally raised questions about the role of the bank.

Bird watched *Prime Time* from the comfort of his sitting-room and was delighted with what he saw. This was the first time that News and Current Affairs had co-operated on an RTE investigation. The collaboration had been awkward at first. Yet, the fact that a major news exposé was followed on the same evening with an analytical *Prime Time* report, would surely have a big impact on public awareness.

The *Prime Time* programme did not end until after 10.00, and when it was over, Lee joined the Current Affairs producers in the hospitality room. He stayed there talking for almost an hour. Then he gathered his belongings and made his way out to the car park. As was to be expected at that hour of the night, there were very few vehicles left. The reporter dug into his pocket, retrieved his key, and inserted it into his car door. Then he froze. The door had already been opened.

He distinctly remembered locking it that morning. He had never failed to lock his car door in the past. Finding it open made him feel very uneasy.

Nothing seemed out of place inside his car and when he noted this, the reporter relaxed. He started his engine and headed towards home. It had been a long day and he was very tired. In such circumstances it was quite possible that his recollection about the morning was faulty. The possibility that he could have left his car open still nagged him however, as he went to sleep that night.

By the following morning, having slept on a bit later than usual, Lee had forgotten about his car-door incident. He turned on the radio as he drove into work. Then he turned down the volume to make a call on his mobile phone. The hands-free car phone unit had never given trouble before. This time, however, it operated as normal for just 20 seconds before the sound from the speaker went dead. It was the first time he had used the hands-free unit since he found the car open the night before.

* * *

The response to the interview with the banker was exactly what the reporters had hoped for. Opposition parties and the Irish Congress of Trade Unions immediately piled on the pressure. They complained about the government response to the story to date.

Labour Party leader, Ruairi Quinn, called for an immediate investigation into the RTE 'allegations'. Democratic Left finance spokesman, Pat Rabbitte, said, 'the saga at NIB is an obscenity against the taxpayer, and the Tanaiste (Mary Harney) must use the Companies Acts to put in an inspector to root out the facts.' Fine Gael Spokesman on Finance, Michael Noonan, demanded that the Chairman of the Revenue Commissioners should answer questions before a Dáil committee because the secret Revenue investigation of NIB 'will not address public concern.'

Derek McDowell of the Labour Party called on NIB's parent, National Australia Bank, to publish the results of its internal investigation into the scheme. He also demanded that the Central Bank Governor, and the Chairman of the Revenue Commissioners, as well as representatives of individual banks, be called before the Select Oireachtas Committee on Finance and General Affairs.

The Irish Congress of Trade Unions demanded legislative changes to tackle fraud and tax evasion. Patricia O'Donovan, Deputy General Secretary of Congress, said, 'the millions of tax being evaded is badly needed to finance essential services for many groups, like people with mental handicap, victims of child abuse, and elderly patients on waiting lists for health care.'

In response to this pressure, the Taoiseach Bertie Ahern, gave an interview. It was the first time he had spoken about the affair, although details of the NIB scheme had been public for four weeks. He insisted that the matter was being fully investigated. If more legislative powers were needed to uncover the full facts, he promised he would provide them. He commented that, 'NIB are a sensible, legal bank and they would have to see to it that any breaches which they have, will have to be dealt with.' The finance editor of *The Irish Times*, Cliff Taylor, remarked, 'perhaps the government is finally realising just how deeply the public feel about the issue of offshore funds, first highlighted in the Ansbacher deposits.' Finance minister, Charlie McCreevy, also issued a statement. He said he regarded the NIB issue as one of serious concern.

Bird and Lee were delighted with all these reactions. The collaboration between News and Current Affairs had produced a perfect result. Economics reporter, Jane Suiter wrote in *The Irish Times* that the pressure on National Irish Bank was intense. She added, 'the Revenue is thought to have moved from an initial examination of the issues with the bank to looking intensely at the scheme in question, how it worked and was marketed.'

In the face of all this reaction, National Irish Bank refused to make any comment. The bank made no attempt to deny the assertions made by the duffle-bag banker, that the holders of illegitimate accounts had been targeted, and that the senior management at the bank must have known about it.

There was just one week to go before the High Court would hear the arguments for and against the continuation of the injunction. The station's lawyers were still pessimistic about RTE's chances of winning. But Bird and Lee were far more confident. They were now sure their reports had hit home. If the public had been made aware that something illegal must have gone on, then surely the judiciary would take note.

* * *

The evening after the interview with the banker had been broadcast, Lee made his way towards the office of Department of Finance in Merrion Street. The Institute of Taxation had complained about new measures proposed for the 1998 Finance Bill, the Bill which would give legal effect to the changes announced in the budget. His plan was to stand in front of the Department of Finance and summarise the complaint made by the taxation institute. He would then rush back to the RTE and compile a report for *Six One*.

Some distance from the Department he exchanged pleasantries with a civil servant whom he knew from the past. Lee had spent two years in the civil service shortly after leaving school. He had fond memories of many who worked there. The civil servant complimented the reporter on his television work, particularly the NIB story. He wanted to know if he was planning to reveal more in the future. When he learned that

Lee was on his way to the Department of Finance, the civil servant became quite excited.

'You will never believe what's been going on there.'

'What?' asked the obviously interested reporter.

The civil servant glanced over his shoulder and looked up and down the street. He satisfied himself that no one was listening. He lowered his voice.

'One hundred and fifty-five files have gone missing,' he said.

'A hundred and fifty-five! What did they relate to?' asked Lee.

'They were requested by the Moriarty Tribunal.'

'They related to Haughey? How do you know?'

'A friend of mine works in the Department. He showed me an internal memo.'

'Do you have the memo?'

'No, but I might be able to get it.'

A second civil servant interrupted the scene and the conversation was abruptly dropped. Lee looked at his watch. He told his old friend he would ring one day and the two of them might go for a pint. Then he headed off towards Merrion Street where his cameraman was already waiting.

By Sunday night, the reporter decided that he simply could not wait any longer. He had to learn more about the missing files. How could such a large amount of material disappear from the Department of Finance? This could have serious repercussions. As a news story it would be significant. He did not know where his civil servant friend lived so he took out the phone book and dialled the numbers of several people who shared the same surname and initial. Eventually, he got lucky and the familiar voice of his friend answered the phone.

They spoke for a while about families and children, and caught up a bit on old times. Then they moved on to talk about NIB. Lee told his friend that himself and Bird had more to reveal. The story was going to get bigger. The civil servant advised him to be careful. With so much at stake, the bank could decide to play dirty. He said a brother of a friend of his had recently been fired by NIB over some internal wrangling. His friend's brother had said the bank could be ruthless when it wanted to be. When the discussion about NIB was exhausted the next topic of conversation needed no introduction.

'Well, anyway.' That was all Lee had to say. The civil servant knew what he meant. It was time to get down to the real reason for the phone call.

'Yeah. You'll never believe it,' started the civil servant. 'The note was issued about three weeks ago.' Then he stopped for one anxious moment. 'Jesus, I hope your phoned isn't tapped.'

'Not at all,' said Lee. 'Don't worry. You're fine. Sure they'd never tap my home phone.' Although Lee said this, he still wasn't sure. The irritating little disruptions on his home telephone line had continued. His car phone had been acting up since he had found his door opened. He had stopped discussing NIB, in detail, over the phone. He had admitted to Bird he was becoming a bit paranoid. If he were to mention any of these factors to his civil servant friend, however, he might scare him off unnecessarily.

'Go on then,' he said, 'what about the files?'

'The note was circulated in the department. It came from a very senior level, a Second Secretary.' The civil servant was being quite precise about what he was saying.

'What was the name of the Second Secretary? asked Lee.

He gave him the name

'Oh, I know who he is,' said Lee.

'Well, the memo said ...'

Suddenly, the civil servant's voice was drowned out by the interference of very loud, very rapid, sharp, pulsing noises on the telephone line. The hair on the back of Lee's neck stood up and the colour drained from his face. The phone connection was lost although the pulsing noises continued to drum into his ear. He put down the receiver and waited 20 seconds. Then he lifted the receiver again and dialled once more. He could hear his friend's voice again. The rapid pulsing noises were still there, although they were quieter this time. The civil servant was clearly frightened and he quickly put down his receiver. Lee ran to his mobile phone and dialled one more time. The line was clear but the civil servant was highly agitated.

'Your phone is tapped! Your phone is tapped!' he said.

Lee did not know what to say. His own pulse was still racing. How could interference like that have come at such a sensitive point in a telephone conversation?

'I'm ringing you on my mobile phone this time. That can't be tapped.'

'Don't be so sure,' the civil servant replied. 'If this story is going to get as big as you say, then anything could be going on .... Look, I think we should leave it for now... I'll contact you in a few weeks.'

Lee's heart sank. He had been on the verge of getting a great story about missing files at the Department of Finance. Now that had been scuppered. He was livid, although he could not blame the civil servant. It had been a very frightening incident. Something very peculiar seemed to be going on.

Five minutes later, Lee's wife, Mary, picked up the home telephone and dialled her mother in Tipperary. The line she got was crystal clear and she stayed talking for more than 20 minutes.

The Practice of Loading

At about the same time as Lee was having trouble with his phone, Bird received a call from the duffle-bag banker. He said he was happy about his interview and about the way his identity had been protected. Yet, he was beginning to worry. The banker suspected that private detectives had been employed by NIB and he feared he might be caught with a duffle bag full of documents. He wanted to get rid of them fast.

He told Bird that his new evidence had nothing to do with the offshore scheme. Instead, it would prove what he had told him at Belfield – that NIB secretly took money out of customer accounts over a number of years. It would confirm the findings of the internal audit report for Carrick-on-Shannon. The practice of taking money from customer accounts 'for no legitimate reason and without customer knowledge' was widespread. He said he had debit slips which would show that it went on in Cork. In addition, he had evidence that NIB deliberately loaded extra fees and charges onto customers for transactions that never took place.

The banker explained that it would take some time to go through all of his documents. He wanted Bird to drive to a hotel in Limerick and book a room for the night. This would minimise the risk of the banker being spotted because he knew nobody there. He said he would meet Bird at the hotel and give him the documents. He thought it would be a good idea for Lee to be there too.

* * *

Bird and Lee arrived at the hotel two hours early. They booked into their rooms and then adjourned to a nearby pub to consider strategy. The focus of their investigation had shifted away from the offshore investment scheme. Now they wanted to tell people that the fourth-largest bank in the country had been stealing money from customer accounts. The internal audit reports for Carrick-on-Shannon and Carndonagh, and the letter from the Walkinstown branch, were very disturbing. The reporters decided that the best approach would be to combine this documentary evidence and a new interview with a banker in a single report. The plan was that Bird would concentrate on the banker while Lee would focus on the documents.

The reporters returned to the hotel at 7.45 in the evening. It was quiet in the lobby at that hour. Nobody took much notice of them as they sat there talking. Nobody took much notice either, at 8.05, when an odd looking man, wearing a navy blue overcoat, sauntered into the hotel. A white plastic bag was tucked under his arm. He glanced at the two journalists as he walked over to the elevator. Then he pushed the up button and waited for the lift to arrive.

'That's him,' whispered Bird looking at Lee but nodding in the direction of the lift.

The two reporters eyed each other. Then they slowly got up from their seats and strolled silently towards the elevator. They stood beside the man and waited for the lift to arrive. When the elevator door opened the three of them got in. Bird pushed the button for the third floor. Two minutes later, after hanging up his coat, the banker settled into an armchair in the reporter's hotel room. Then he opened his white plastic bag and began to distribute the documents.

* * *

He started with an internal memo dated 21 May 1990. It had been issued by the General Manager of NIB, Frank Brennan. This was in response to the internal audit report for Carrick-on-Shannon, dated April of that year. The report had highlighted 'that interest charges were increased without legitimate reason or customers' knowledge on twenty accounts in November 1989 and thirty-three accounts in February 1990.' This memo from Brennan was addressed to Kevin Curran, the regional manager in charge of the area. Brennan wrote: 'Given that the auditors found 33 cases of loading it would appear that that branch have used the "soft option principle" widely and this is unacceptable.'

The reporters noted that the General Manager of NIB did not say that the money which had been stolen should be repaid to the customers. They also noted that Brennan had used the term 'soft option principle' to describe the theft. The fact that the bank had a special term for the practice surprised them. It suggested that this form of stealing may not have been such an unusual occurrence.

The next memo produced by the banker came from NIB's Chief Executive at the time, Jim Lacey. He, too, was responding to the internal audit report for Carrick-on-Shannon. Lacey's memo was addressed to

Brennan and it was also dated 21 May. The Chief Executive said that interest-loading on customer accounts should be stopped. However, he did not say that the money which had been taken should be paid back.

The reporters were amazed by the next batch of pages produced by the banker. He had a bunch of internal NIB debit slips from the branch at Carrick-on-Shannon. He also had copies of several bank giro credit slips from the same NIB branch.

The first giro he handed over was dated 22 February 1990. This was the day, according to the internal auditors, that 33 customer accounts had been raided by the management of the branch. The giro was made out for £1,685. Attached to it was a calculator receipt showing the 33 separate amounts which went to make up this total. They varied from £20 to £150. The average was £51. This was the money which had been illegitimately and secretly taken from the customer accounts. The giro showed that this stolen money was transferred into an internal branch account, the number of which was 490 11 269. The name given to this internal account was 'Interest Charged on Current Account'.

The banker then handed over several other giro slips made out to the exact same internal account. The dates of these other giro slips ranged over a number of years. This implied that the practice of loading, highlighted by the auditors in April 1990, had in fact been going on for a very long time.

One of the giros was dated January 1987. It was made out for £1,125. A calculator receipt showed that this amount came from a raid on 21 accounts. The amounts taken ranged from as little as £25 to as much as £150. The term 'loading' was clearly written on the giro slip.

Another giro, dated May 1987, suggested a similar story. A total of £1,615.90 had been taken from 21 customers. The banker also produced copies of 14 of the 21 internal branch debit slips used by the bank to steal this money. All of these debit slips were filled out in the same handwriting. Each one carried a code number: 76. The information on the slips included the name of each account, the number of each account, and the amount of money which was taken by the bank. None of these debit slips had been signed by customers but all had been stamped by the bank.

The same pattern was repeated again and again. In November 1987, the amount on the giro was £654.48. In May 1988, 14 customers were debited by a total of £1,096. In November 1988, £1,191 was taken from 24 customers. In May 1989, it was £2,477 from 29 accounts. In August 1989 the total taken was £1,229.

Each time the money was taken from the accounts of these customers it was transferred into the same internal branch account, numbered 490 11 269. All of the money in this account went to boost the bank's profits.

It was clear that senior management at the bank including the Chief Executive, Jim Lacey, and the General Manager, Frank Brennan, had been told about Carrick-on-Shannon. It was also clear that neither of them demanded that the money be repaid to the customers. However, the duffle-bag banker's white plastic bag carried some more devastating information. He took out a document which showed that despite being pulled up by the internal auditors, John O'Reilly, the manager at Carrick-on-Shannon, received high marks for his performance in 1990. As a result, O'Reilly was rewarded with a healthy Christmas bonus of £1,750. It seemed that he had not been disciplined for his actions.

The white plastic bag contained a lot of other documents too. The banker had brought wads of internal debit slips from the NIB branch in Cork. These followed the exact same pattern as the debit slips from Carrick-on-Shannon. They carried the customer name, the account number, and the now familiar code number 76. Again, none of the slips had been signed by the customers but all had been stamped by the bank. The debit slips from the Cork branch were dated May and November 1988, May and November 1989, and May 1990.

In each case, the debits were totalled up and transferred by bank giro into an internal branch account. What was surprising, however, was that the name and number of the internal branch account used in Cork was the exact same as had been used in Carrick-on-Shannon. The name was 'Interest Charged on Current Account'. The number was 490 11 269. A total of £8,276 had been transferred by giro into this account in Cork during November 1989. Another £8,566 was transferred the following May.

The amounts on the individual debit slips were larger for Cork than for Carrick-on-Shannon. Figures from £50 to £500 were common. There were also some odd amounts such as £327, £239, and £267. One business account was debited by a massive £2,826 in one go.

There were other names on debit slips which the reporters could not make out because of the handwriting. They noticed, however, that a lot of the accounts, had been loaded repeatedly.

Taking Cork and Carrick-on-Shannon together, the total number of debit slips produced by the banker exceeded 120. Lee scanned through them all. When he was finished he addressed the banker.

'Were these debit slips recorded as withdrawals on the customer statements printed out by the bank computer?'

'Yes, they were,' replied the banker.

'So how did the bank get away with it?' This had been puzzling Lee from the beginning.

'The computer-generated bank statements were changed,' said the banker.

'Changed?'

'Yes. Changed. They were intercepted before they were posted out. They originally showed a deduction for legitimate interest, and a separate withdrawal for the illegitimate interest. The customers would have noticed. So these two figures were added together. The total was then included as a single interest charge on a new bank statement which had to be typed up.'

'So it wasn't computer-generated?'

'No,' replied the banker. 'It had to be manually typed.'

'And the customers would never spot it?' Lee was amazed by what he was hearing.

'Practically never,' replied the banker. 'The calculation of interest on overdrafts is far too difficult for most people to follow. That's why it was so easy for the bank to get away with it.'

'And what happened to the computer statements?' asked the reporter.

'They were kept in the branch and eventually thrown in the bin.'

When the banker finished explaining about interest-loading he started to explain about fees. He said another way in which NIB took money from customers was by loading or charging them with extra fees for phantom banking transactions such as lodgements, withdrawals and other services. These bogus fees were also deducted from customer accounts without their knowledge.

The banker produced a sizeable portion of a computer printout for the NIB branch at College Green in Dublin. The printout showed that, in that branch, in one quarter alone, fees were adjusted and charged to the accounts of over 1,000 customers out of a total of 1,700. The windfall to the bank at the stroke of a pen was about £15,000. One business customer in particular had been levied £1,237 in adjusted charges in that period. Personal accounts were adjusted by smaller amounts. In some cases, the bank went to the bother for just a few pence.

The banker explained that while some of these fee adjustments may have been for legitimate reasons, the vast majority had been added arbitrarily. He also said that the customers were never notified about the bogus fees being charged. The banker knew of some cases where NIB branches had doubled their fee income through this practice of arbitrary fee loading. He said it was widespread throughout the NIB branch network, and had been going on for years.

The reporters were astonished that one individual banker could have amassed such incriminating evidence. The publication of the documentation he had collected would devastate the bank. It would appear that friendly bank managers had been stealing from customer accounts for years. They gave the money they stole to their employer, who kept it and did not discipline the managers. Instead, they were rewarded for their thievery with large Christmas bonuses.

Most people consider banks to be trustworthy and reputable. However, what had gone on at National Irish Bank had the potential to bring the entire Irish banking industry into disrepute. Ordinary bank customers all over the country were likely to start questioning the integrity of their local bank manager.

* * *

The banker was visibly tired by the time he had finished with his documents. It had taken him more than an hour to go through the contents of his white plastic bag. The two journalists were grateful, yet they had one more favour to ask him.

Bird looked at the banker. 'Do you know what we need now?' he said.

'What?' inquired the banker.

'We need another interview with an insider, someone with first-hand experience, a person who can explain how all of these practices worked.'

There was a moment of silence as the banker looked back at Bird. It was obvious that the reporters wanted him to do the interview.

'It would be the same as before,' urged Bird. 'We'd hide your face and get an actor for your voice.'

Another silence passed as the banker gave the matter more thought. Then he breathed out heavily.

'Okay. I'll do it. I might as well get it all over with.'

'Great,' said Bird, the relief clearly visible on his face.

'When will we do it?' asked the banker.

'As soon as possible,' replied the reporter. 'What about tomorrow?'

Arrangements were made for the banker to come to Bird's hotel room at half past ten the following morning. The room did not have to be vacated until midday. This would allow Bird an hour and a half for the interview. A late-night phone call to the news desk ensured that a cameraman would arrive in the foyer of the hotel half an hour before the banker.

* * *

The second interview with the duffle-bag banker lasted 55 minutes. He outlined how bank officials targeted the customers for whom they would fill out bogus debit slips. Those who were demanding, or troublesome, were likely to be picked. So also were customers who constantly exceeded their overdraft limits. In all situations, however, the banker said there was no legitimate reason why any customer was picked. The aim of the exercise was to increase the income and the profitability of the bank.

There was nothing scientific about the amounts by which each account was raided. The figures were just plucked out of the air. You could have a situation where a business customer was paying anything up to £4,000 in hidden interest charges in any one year. According to the banker, it was common knowledge that some people who engaged in this practice were subsequently promoted within the bank.

The banker admitted that he personally had engaged in the practice of interest-loading. He said his superiors at the bank had instructed him to do it. They got him to fill out debit slips to steal money out of customer accounts. His bosses got him to cover up by intercepting computerised bank statements and replacing them with false, manually typed statements.

Interest-loading was a difficult practice to eliminate. If customers noticed their interest charges fell during a period of stagnant interest rates, then they might begin to ask questions. The banker said that it was common knowledge within NIB that this 'soft option principle' was used. Yet, he was not aware of any official who was ever reprimanded or disciplined as a result.

The interviewee went on to say that the second practice, fee-loading, occurred in the vast majority of NIB branches. The bank earned millions of pounds this way, from the early 1980s until at least the middle of the 1990s. Customers were never made aware of what was going on. The extra fees charged were just 'plucked from the sky'. He added that: 'From the perspective of bank personnel, the only justification (for the fee loading) was that the money was going on to the bank's bottom line.

It wasn't seen as "ripping off" as such. No individual was actually ripping off a customer. The money was going into the bank's coffers.'

The banker admitted that he had also engaged in the practice of fee-loading.

> I increased the fees in the same way as other officials. I had targets to achieve and it was basically to increase the income for the bank .... If it was a legitimate charge, the increase in the fee should have been negotiated with the customer prior to the charging period, and communicated with the customer. But again, like the 'current account interest,' the 'soft option' was taken ... and you hoped the customer didn't query it.

> There was extreme pressure on branch managers to increase their fee income and their interest income. League tables were prepared by senior management in the bank, highlighting the top achievers in this area. People at the bottom of the ladder felt pressurised.

> At the beginning of each financial year, targets were set by the senior management of the bank for each individual branch. Each branch was given a specific target for fee income and it was a figure which you had to achieve, or exceed, at the end of the year. You would break that down into a quarterly figure, and in adjusting your fees you would be mindful of the fact that there was a certain level of fee income that you had to attain. You kept that figure in mind, and you worked your increases in to ensure that the figure was achieved, or in some cases exceeded. There was considerable pressure at the time to increase the fee income. It was seen as a very important area of profitability for the bank ... there was no legitimate reason (for the loading) other than that pressure was on the branch manager to achieve a certain level of fee income.

* * *

The consequences for NIB of the scandal which the banker had outlined could not be more serious. Since the RTE reporters had to explain it to the public, they decided that they had better do it comprehensively. Instinctively, both Bird and Lee knew that an ordinary television news report would not be adequate to explain the full details of this new scandal. Their best hope would be to aim for a very long news report, and also to bring *Prime Time* in on these latest revelations. Ed Mulhall had no problem agreeing to a long news report, and *Prime Time* was enthusiastic about participating again.

One thing, however, nagged at Bird and Lee. It was that the scandal was almost becoming too serious. The duffle-bag banker had been reliable and straight. He had produced documents to back up everything he had said. The practices he had recounted were totally disgraceful. They had the potential, if explained properly, to cause a mini-run on the fourth-largest bank in the country. The two reporters, and their boss, began to get nervous about the full consequences of the new story they were now in a position to tell.

To be on the safe side, Mulhall insisted that more corroboration should be sought. Everything the banker had outlined would have to be confirmed by other NIB insiders. If the practices he spoke about were widespread, then surely other bankers would be prepared to confess. Mulhall recommended that the reporters should also search for a second interviewee.

Bird and Lee started to check back with all of their sources. Up until now, they had only discussed the offshore investment scheme with the NIB insiders. They were surprised with the reaction they got when they brought up the subject of loading interest and fees on to unsuspecting customers.

Several NIB managers, and some former managers, openly admitted to the practices. They confirmed that fee-loading was widespread and all of them had participated in it. Some of them insisted that they never got involved in the practice of interest-loading. Yet all of them said that they knew it went on.

A big test came when Bird, using his alias, Joe McGrath, phoned an employee who was once an NIB internal auditor. The former auditor was nervous but he was an honest man. He confirmed that fee loading was widespread and that it went on for many years. He also confirmed that the interest loading practice, whereby false debit slips were secretly filled out, had been common. This NIB employee complained that the audit division had been starved of resources and had frequently been unable to do its job properly.

By this stage, the two reporters had been talking to staff, and to former staff, of NIB for a month and a half. Most of their contacts had seen how one of their colleagues had been disguised on the News and on *Prime Time* the previous week. Because of this, the search for a second interviewee was much easier than either Bird or Lee had expected. Two days after interviewing the duffle-bag banker in a hotel in Limerick, Bird interviewed another NIB manager in Dublin. The location again was a hotel room and the interview lasted for 15 minutes.

* * *

The Dublin-based manager who agreed to be interviewed had considerable experience of the NIB branch network. Bird showed him the internal audit report for Carndonagh which highlighted how interest charges were loaded at that branch in 1989 and 1990.

'Are you familiar with reports like this?' asked Bird.

'Yes,' said the banker.

'In this particular case, it says loading will be discontinued from 1990. Do you believe it went on after 1990?'

'Yes,' said the banker again.

'Why do you believe that?' asked the reporter.

'I would be fairly confident that the same line would be taken in the following audit report that was done on that particular branch,' replied the interviewee.

'Do you have personal knowledge that it went on after 1990?'

'Yes,' he said.

'The bank was saying this practice must be stopped. You're saying it continued.'

'Yes.'

'How widespread do you think current account interest loading was?'

'I'd be surprised if it didn't happen in every branch in the country,' said the NIB banker. His tone was unequivocal.

This second interviewee also spoke about the way bogus fees were loaded onto unsuspecting customers. He said, 'the thinking was that in 95 per cent of the cases (the extra fees) would not be questioned' by customers. 'It was a culture. I think it was just something that people were reared with. Obviously, there was big pressure from senior management on branch staff to get their fee income up. Every branch was a profit centre in its own right. The manager's performance was based on the profit that he generated at the end of the year. Fee income was a big addition to his bottom line.'

This new banker admitted on camera that he, too, had loaded illegitimate fees onto customer accounts. 'It was something I didn't really think about. It was something that I had seen through my years.'

Bird showed him the computer printout of fee amendments for the NIB branch at College Green in Dublin. He asked the expert to explain how it was done.

'They could be amended within a certain timescale. A computer amendment was made and the amended figure would be charged to the account,' responded the banker.

The reporter pushed harder. 'So take a couple of hours and what? ... I mean what type of money do you think was being added.'

'A branch could double their fee income.' The banker was definite about what he was saying. 'Everybody was aware that everybody else was doing it.'

A Tilt in Favour
of Press Freedom

THURSDAY, 26 FEBRUARY 1988

On the same day the Dublin-based banker was interviewed by Bird, the High Court finally considered the NIB injunction against RTE. The temporary restraining order had been in operation since 30 January. Under its terms, the national broadcaster was prevented 'howsoever, from making any use whatsoever' of any documentation or information tending to identify NIB customers, accounts, transactions, or investments. When the bank applied for this order, it could not have known that the RTE investigations would go so far. As a result, the arguments for and against the injunction were specific to the bank's controversial offshore investment scheme. The fact that RTE was preparing to reveal an even bigger scandal was irrelevant to the hearing.

RTE's lawyers thought the presence of the two journalists in court could serve as a distraction, so Bird and Lee stayed away. The presiding judge, the late Mr Justice Peter Shanley, listened at length to the arguments on both sides. He summarised the case succinctly:

> RTE has in its possession, information or documents which are secret and concern the business of NIB. NIB say they are not certain as to the nature and the extent of the information in the possession of RTE but ... it is submitted that such information clearly has the necessary character of confidence about it. The bank say they do not know how RTE came to be in possession of the information ... which is not in the public domain, and which the bank has not authorised RTE to use, and which they are entitled to enjoin RTE from using ... RTE concedes that the publication of such information would, in ordinary circumstances, amount to a breach of confidence but ... says there is a compelling public interest in favour of publication in the present case because the information discloses the bank's complicity in a scheme designed to evade tax.

Mr Justice Shanley indicated that it would take him some time to decide on the case. He reserved his judgment.

* * *

The story about NIB stealing money from customer accounts was shelved while the judge was making up his mind. Although there were no legal restrictions preventing the journalists from broadcasting the new story, RTE took the view that it would be disrespectful to the courts to do so before Mr Justice Shanley had finished his work. As a result, Bird embarked on a short holiday, happy in the knowledge that the investigation was on hold. While he was away, Lee prepared a new report for *Prime Time* as well as working on the extended report for news.

The drill was the same as before. The original interview tapes would be used for the news report. Any identifying features of the interviewees were blurred over. The voices of two actors were recorded to disguise those of the bankers. Video graphic representations of some of the internal bank memos were prepared. New camera shots of various NIB branches were ordered.

For the purposes of his second *Prime Time* report, Lee teamed up with Annette Kinne of Andec Communications in Dun Laoghaire. The reporter had worked with Kinne during his early days in Current Affairs, when she, too, had been an RTE employee. He quickly re-established a very good working relationship with the now independent television producer.

The style of the Current Affairs report was dictated by *Prime Time's* executive producer, Eamon O'Connor. Again, he saw no value in using blurred-over interview tapes in a long television report. Instead, *Prime Time* decided to film re-enactments of the interviews with the bankers. This time, however, there would be no silhouettes. The actors' faces could be shown.

The preparations were intense. Lee and Kinne frequently stayed working at Andec's offices until two and three in the morning. Their time was spent sifting through the huge range of documentation, as well as the long interviews with the bankers. They had to work out the very best way to explain the new scandal. They scripted the story 12 different times. Every visual detail of the report was planned in advance, including cameras, lights, actors and props.

The new *Prime Time* and News reports were originally targeted for broadcast during the second week of March. It was hoped that the issue of the injunction would be settled before then. This broadcast schedule, however, was thrown into disarray on the morning of Friday 6 March, when Mr Justice Shanley announced that he had come to a decision.

* * *

RTE's lawyers had consciously played down their chances of a win. This pessimism was based purely on historical precedent. The courts had traditionally favoured the 'preservation of confidence' over the 'public interest in disclosure'. Consequently, there was much surprise in the courtroom when Mr Justice Shanley read out his judgment.

He started by saying that: 'NIB has satisfied me that the publication of the information (in RTE's possession) may well have an adverse effect on its relations with its customers ... the effect ... cannot be quantified in damages. Damages are therefore not an adequate remedy.'

However, he went on to point out that the charges made by RTE:

> could not be more explicit or serious ... RTE draws attention to the fact that the money of the customer ends up back in NIB on deposit earning the same interest rate which it had done before the investment was made. It says there is no reason whatsoever for a customer to invest in such a scheme other than to avail of the anonymity and therefore the tax evasion potential of the scheme. I am quite satisfied that the public interest defence which has been raised on this application has not been raised frivolously and that RTE has made out a strong case. It is clear that RTE proposes to stand over its allegations, and I am satisfied that in such circumstances I should allow the publication of the confidential information preferring, as I do, the public interest in the disclosure of such information as against the interest in preserving its confidence ... I will discharge the *ex parte* injunction.

It looked as if all of the work had paid off but it was far too soon to celebrate. RTE may have won the battle but they had not yet won the war. NIB indicated immediately that it would appeal the verdict to the Supreme Court. This meant the injunction would remain effective until the Supreme Court made a decision.

* * *

RTE's legal team had mushroomed in size by 4.00 that afternoon. A total of seven lawyers settled around the table in the News conference room. They were there to consider the implications of the Supreme Court appeal. Kevin Feeney was still the lead counsel but John Trainor, another senior counsel was drafted in as well. Lee, Mulhall and Eamon O'Connor listened carefully as the lawyers thrashed out a strategy.

The Supreme Court had decided that the issue of the injunction was a very urgent matter. As a result, the five judges had immediately cleared their schedules for the following Friday to listen to both sides of the argument. The speed with which these five had responded suggested that theirs would be a landmark decision.

The lawyers gave some consideration to the new details which the journalists wanted to report. They were disturbed by the findings of the NIB internal auditors and they accepted that a report about these findings would not be a breach of the injunction. However, they strongly recommended that no such report should be broadcast until the Supreme Court had ruled on the appeal. This posed a difficulty because although everyone knew when the appeal would be heard, nobody could tell how long it would take for a decision to be handed down.

* * *

Bird was back from holiday in plenty of time for the appeal, so he and Lee decided to attend the hearing. They arrived, slightly late, and quietly took seats at the back of the courtroom. Richard Nesbitt SC was outlining the case for the bank when they walked in. His arguments were the same as those he had used in the High Court. Mr Justice O'Flaherty, Mr Justice Barrington, Mr Justice Keane and Mr Justice Lynch, as well as the Chief Justice, Liam Hamilton, listened closely to what Nesbitt was saying. These judges let nothing slip past them.

Nesbitt concentrated on the breach of confidence and the damage which the publication of customer names would do to the bank. He outlined NIB's insistence that it did not collude with tax evaders, and that there was no evidence to prove that it did. He also threw in NIB's claim that it had no intention of covering up, or defending, any wrongdoing. He asserted that RTE could decide to publish a list of the names of the offshore investors. If this happened, the barrister claimed, no amount of monetary compensation could possibly remedy the long-term damage that would be inflicted on his client.

The judges did not allow NIB's barrister to have a free run. They quizzed him about the way the offshore scheme worked and they noted that the only advantage it seemed to offer was anonymity from the Revenue Commissioners.

In response, Nesbitt made a big deal of the fact that NIB was already co-operating fully with the Revenue Commissioners and with the Central Bank. Both of these institutions were important arms of the State. They were empowered to fully investigate the scheme and they would do so in private. As a result there was no just cause for any further publicity. All wrongdoings, if indeed any had occurred, would be uncovered and dealt with by the appropriate authorities, not by RTE. The barrister put heavy emphasis on how willingly the bank was co-operating with the ongoing investigations. He stressed that NIB had been co-operating with the Central Bank since they were contacted about the matter a few days before 23 January, the day RTE first broke the story.

At the back of the courtroom, Lee felt a sense of betrayal over what Nesbitt had said. He had arranged a confidential meeting with a Central Banker several days before the first broadcast. He had told him, in very strict confidence, of the details RTE was planning to report. Lee had discussed the merits of such a meeting in advance with his boss, Ed Mulhall. Like RTE, the Central Bank is a semi-state body and the reporter did not want to catch it off-guard with a big breaking story. On the basis of what Nesbitt had told the court however, he began to worry that someone within the Central Bank could have told NIB what RTE was planning.

Bird and Lee were impressed with the sharpness and the intelligent wit displayed throughout the appeal by the Chief Justice, Liam Hamilton. Before this hearing, RTE had refused to confirm for the bank, or for anyone else, precisely what the journalists knew. If they had a full list of investors then NIB might have something to worry about. The Chief Justice, however, would allow none of this ambiguity. He forced RTE's barrister, Kevin Feeney, to divulge the full extent of what the reporters knew about the investors. 'The account numbers of twenty accounts ... and the names of six customers.' When this was revealed it became clear to the court that some of the fears expressed by NIB had been overstated.

* * *

One week later, on the morning of Friday 20 March, Bird and Lee arrived at the Supreme Court to hear the verdict. On this occasion however, they got there in plenty of time. They had spent the previous week checking and re-checking all of their facts. They had tightened the scripts and weeded through the interviews with the bankers. Lee had also spent many more hours in Dun Laoghaire working on *Prime Time* with Annette Kinne. A group of actors had played out the parts of the bankers and the customers on a set designed as a bank. Almost all of the filming that would be required had already been done. Regardless of what the

Supreme Court had decided, the journalists knew they only had to wait five days to reveal their new story.

Each of the five Supreme Court judges wore grave expressions as they took their seats at the bench. Both legal teams, as well as representatives for the bank, RTE and other organs of the media, waited in silence for what had obviously been a difficult decision. Within seconds it became clear that there was a difference of opinion among the judges. Chief Justice Hamilton announced that he was in agreement with the decision which would be read out by Mr Justice Keane. Then Mr Justice O'Flaherty and Mr Justice Barrington said they were in agreement with the judgment which would be read out by Mr Justice Lynch.

The minority judgment was the first to be read out. Mr Justice Keane's opinion was:

> ... the postures adopted by the bank and RTE respectively are not fully justified. The bank's claim to restrain RTE from making any use whatsoever of the confidential information obtained by them ... goes too far. So too does the claim of RTE to be entitled to make whatever use they wish of the information .... The existence of an efficient banking system based on a confidential relationship between the individual banks and their customers is a central feature of a modern economy. To give to RTE unfettered licence to publish the names of every customer involved in the CMI scheme ... would be to effect a major inroad into that confidential relationship, which is warranted neither by principle nor authority .... It is undoubtedly the case that, at this stage of the proceedings RTE cannot be said to have done anything which is an invasion of the plaintiff's [NIB] rights ... RTE steadfastly refused to give any undertaking whatever inhibiting their future course of conduct in relation to the confidential information in their possession, no doubt for what seem to them good reasons. It is a necessary consequence of that attitude, however, that the court enjoys jurisdiction to grant a *quia timet* injunction.

The effect of this verdict, if it had been approved by more than two of the judges, would have been that RTE could only publicise NIB customer details under very restrictive conditions. They would have to be sure that the customer had been, or was planning to, evade tax. In addition, they would have to inform the Revenue Commissioners, the bank, and the customers, in advance. At least seven days ahead of publication, RTE would effectively have to invite the bank and its customers to apply to the courts for a restraining order preventing such publication.

One of the most positive elements of this minority opinion was that the Chief Justice and Mr Justice Keane concluded that the investigation which had been conducted by RTE had been legitimately undertaken. They also insisted that the two reporters should not be restrained from using confidential information to pursue their investigation.

The decision of the majority of the bench was delivered without any delay by Mr Justice Lynch:

> It is said that the proper course for RTE is to furnish such information as they have to the regulatory authorities and no further. I certainly agree that RTE should furnish their information to such authorities and especially if they are asked for such information by such authorities but the allegation which they make is of serious tax evasion and this is a matter of genuine interest and importance to the general public and especially to the vast majority who are law abiding taxpayers and I am satisfied that it is in the public interest that the general public should be given this information.
>
> I have no problem therefore in upholding the refusal of the learned trial judge to grant the injunction ... if RTE decide to publish the names of any investors they should be very sure and should take all necessary steps to ensure that they do not publish the names of innocent investors.

There was jubilation in the RTE camp on hearing this verdict. The highest judges in the land had decided that the details the reporters had uncovered were so serious that they were prepared to set a new precedent. The public's right to know was judged more important than NIB's right to protect the confidential relationship it had built up with tax evaders. The courts had asserted that RTE had not put a foot wrong to date. Bird and Lee had not infringed the rights of the bank. Their investigation was legitimate.

An editorial in *The Irish Times* welcomed the outcome which, it said, represented:

> a significant tilt by the courts in favour of press freedom ... an encouraging signal that it (the Supreme Court) also recognises that the public interest can be served by investigative journalism .... The Supreme Court ruling should concentrate the minds of policy makers. They have obdurately refused to amend the State's penal libel laws and seem content with a situation in which journalists operate within one of the most restrictive legal environments in the developed world.

In the same newspaper, Marie McGonagle, a university specialist in media law, analysed the verdict. She said it was a decision which enhanced the reputation of the press and the judiciary. McGonagle wrote that, 'the court made it clear that what it was vindicating was responsible journalism'.

While these reactions were being written, National Irish Bank was composing a response of its own. In an act which must rank among one of the most brazen attempts to put a spin on a media story, NIB went all out to welcome the verdict. At six minutes to five on the evening of the verdict, the bank issued the following public statement:

SUPREME COURT DECISION

We are pleased that innocent customers have been protected by the Supreme Court judgement which has upheld the principle of customer confidentiality. Customers entrust confidential information about their corporate and personal affairs to Banks. It is important that customers can continue to rely on Bank confidentiality in relation to their financial affairs. Tax compliant investors in products sold by CMI through NIB in Ireland are entitled to confidentiality and to maintenance of their good name. In taking this action, NIB has sought only to protect these rights and at no stage has attempted to inhibit legitimate public comment on issues arising from the sale of CMI products in Ireland.

ENDS   **20th March 1998**

The first the RTE reporters knew of the NIB spin, was when Ted Harding, a reporter with the *Sunday Business Post*, phoned Lee to get a response. Harding had not been present in court for the judgment and believed that NIB's response meant that RTE had lost. Bird, Lee and Mulhall were finalising a detailed list of questions to be put to NIB about stealing from customer accounts when the phone call from the *Sunday Business Post* came through.

'That was a bit of hard luck in court,' said Harding.

'What do you mean, hard luck?' Lee was surprised.

'You lost.'

'Lost? We didn't lose. We won. Hands down.' Lee was very puzzled. Ted Harding is an excellent journalist. There had to be a good reason why he had got it so wrong.

'But NIB has issued a statement,' said Harding, equally puzzled. 'They have welcomed the judgment.'

'They have?' Lee was amazed.

'Yeah,' said Harding. 'The NIB statement says the court decision has upheld the principle of customer confidentiality.'

'Well, you have to admire them for brass neck,' said Lee. Then he proceeded to explain the two verdicts to the newspaper journalist.

As a result of Harding's phone call, Ed Mulhall contacted the RTE publicity department to confirm that the station was issuing its own press release about the Supreme Court judgment.

* * *

Despite NIB's attempt to claim victory, the judgment of the Supreme Court was well noted at the Department of Enterprise and Employment. There, the Minister of State for Science, Technology, and Commerce, Noel Treacy, had spent almost two months apparently sitting on the fence. He had known for 50 days that NIB did not have the necessary government authorisation for the launch of CMI products. This meant that the sale of the offshore investment scheme had been illegal. Whatever he was doing behind the scenes, the Minister had taken no obvious action to deal with this offence. Now the Supreme Court had deemed the details of the scheme important enough to outweigh the bank's right to confidentiality. The minister had to react. Preparations were finalised for an officer of his department to be authorised, the following Monday, under the 1989 Insurance Act. A government officer was finally going to be sent into NIB to investigate the offshore scheme.

Finishing Touches

1.00 P.M., SATURDAY, 21 MARCH 1998

Lee drove towards the city the day after the Supreme Court judgment. The reporter had arranged to meet Bird at RTE for some last-minute planning. They also wanted to re-check the letter they would be jointly sending to NIB the following Monday. A face-to-face meeting was the safest way to deal with these issues. Lately, the telephone conversations between the two reporters had become very short affairs. They had grown more wary about discussing NIB details on the phone after Lee had experienced a second disturbing incident two weeks previously.

It happened after he had phoned his mother from home. His conversation lasted about ten minutes. A short time later, he had dialled a number in Dun Laoghaire to enquire about a pest-control service. A few minutes into this second conversation, he was interrupted by the sound of his mobile phone ringing. Lee cut short his call to Dun Laoghaire to answer the mobile call. His mother was on the line in an agitated state. She explained that she had forgotten to tell him something earlier and had phoned him back a few minutes after their previous conversation had ended. She had discovered that his home line was busy, yet she had still been able to hear everything he was saying to the service provider in Dun Laoghaire. Lee's mother had made several unsuccessful attempts to interrupt that conversation before concluding that hers was not a typical crossed-line experience. She was disturbed by the incident and warned her son to be careful about what he was saying on his home telephone.

The reporter decided to play down the affair. He feared people might consider him paranoid if he made much of the incident. Bird and Mulhall were the only two people he had told about it. They agreed that it provided yet another reason for caution.

Now however, as he drove towards RTE in the sunshine, interference on his telephone line was the last thing on the reporter's mind. His number one priority was to ensure, along with Bird, Mulhall and Eamon Kennedy that there were no last-minute hiccups. Most important of all was to ensure that every possible legal loose end was tied up. The lawyers had advised that nothing should be included in the reports unless the journalists had strong documentary evidence to back it up. Regardless of how convincing the bankers had been in their interviews, none of their comments could be used without a corroborating piece of paper. As a result, the extent to which fee-loading occurred at the bank would have to be played down. This illicit practice was obvious from the computer printout for College Green, but it had not been noted in any of the internal audit reports. Hence, the reporters had been instructed to minimise their explanation of the extent to which customers were robbed by way of bogus fees and charges.

Lee's concentration on all these matters was broken by the sound of his car phone ringing. His hands-free phone unit had righted itself temporarily a few days after his first *Prime Time* report. This unit had malfunctioned the morning after he had found his car door open in the outer RTE car park. A specialist had checked out the sound problem which resulted. He had confirmed that there was nothing wrong with the car phone speaker but was unable to explain why the unit had malfunctioned. It was working now, however. Lee pushed the answer button. It was Bird on the line. The older reporter sounded troubled.

'They're following me,' he said.

'Who is?' asked Lee noting the uneasiness in Bird's voice.

'I don't know who they are.'

'How do you know they're following you so?'

'I just know that they are.'

'How?' Lee noted that the traffic lights ahead had switched to red and he slowed to a stop.

'I got a call from a source. They're on to us. I'm telling you.' Bird sounded definite.

'Who's on to us?'

'The bank, I suppose, my caller wasn't specific.'

'He didn't say it was the bank though, did he?' Lee was reluctant to jump to conclusions.

'No, but I saw them,' said Bird.

'Who did you see?'

'I saw who was following me. There was a cream-coloured Hiace van outside my house this morning. I've seen that same van several times today.'

Lee was silent. He noted the seriousness in Bird's voice but he didn't know what to say. Perhaps Bird was getting carried away. There were vans everywhere. He could even see a white van in his own rear-view mirror.

'They're probably following you too.' The concern was obvious in the older reporter's voice.

'You can't be serious.' Lee was shocked at the thought.

'You'd never know. Just in case, keep an eye out for a cream-coloured van. You can't see one near you now, can you?'

'There is a van behind me all right but it's not cream. It's white, dirty white. In fact, it's filthy white.'

'That's it!' exclaimed Bird, all shocked.

Lee said nothing. He just looked in his mirror.

'What does the driver look like? Has he got a beard?' asked Bird.

'He's kind of youngish. Yeah, he's got a big beard all right, but he's also got a child in the front seat beside him. So it can't be him.'

'That's him! That's him!' Bird's concern could almost be mistaken for excitement. 'There was a child in the van this morning as well.'

Lee was startled. He said nothing.

'They must be after you too,' said Bird. 'He probably brought the kid along as a cover.'

Lee was lost for words. 'God!' was all he could manage to say.

'He must have been outside your house too,' added Bird.

'I didn't see him,' replied Lee. He was a bit shocked now himself and had not noticed that the traffic lights had turned from red to green. The reporter was still concentrating on his rear-view mirror.

The beep of a car horn brought him to his senses. He put his car into gear, about to take off. The horn sounded again, longer this time.

'Ah, shag off and wait,' he said out loud, and he began to pull away from the traffic lights. His mood had become very serious.

The horn sounded once more. It was coming from the outside lane. Lee glanced over to see who was being so impatient. That was when he saw Bird happily driving his silver-coloured Opel Vectra. His window was down and he was roaring laughing at the good of his own joke. He had been driving behind Lee all along and couldn't resist the opportunity to make light of the reporters' concern about surveillance. He was wearing sun glasses and that was why the dirty-white Hiace van appeared cream to him.

'Mind they don't catch you,' he continued, laughing heartily.

Lee laughed. He had never thought of Bird as a practical joker.

'I'll get you back!' he shouted.

The horn of the Vectra was sounded once more before the older reporter sped off in the fast lane. He was still laughing when Lee caught up with him in the car park at RTE. By that stage the white Hiace van had long disappeared in the direction of Blackrock.

* * *

Early on Monday morning, the two reporters got down to the serious business of contacting NIB. Their biggest fear was that the bank might apply to court for another restraining order. NIB might like to claim that they were not given enough time to check out the very damaging allegations about to be broadcast. If such a claim was credible then the bank could possibly succeed in getting another temporary restraining order. The reporters had seen how long it took to deal with the previous injunction and did not want to go through that same process again. To minimise the risk of this happening, the letter being sent by the reporters was very specific. The details of what they were going to allege, and where the bank could find the evidence for these allegations, were spelt out as much as possible. The letter which was delivered by courier to NIB's chief operations officer Philip Halpin read as follows:

Dear Mr Halpin,

RTE's is working on a story for transmission on Wednesday 25th March in our News and Current Affairs programmes concerning National Bank's retail banking operations.

In order to assist us to present a fair and accurate report on this issue we would be obliged if you could provide answers to the following questions.

1. RTE understands that internal Audit Reports in 1990 for the Carndonagh and Carrick-on-Shannon branches of NIB revealed that interest charges were increased without legitimate reason and without customer knowledge.
– Is this true?
– If it is true what action did the bank take?
– Were the customers so affected notified and re-imbursed?

2. We also understand that interest loading occurred in Walkinstown in 1989 and in Cork in 1988, 1989, and 1990.
– Is this true?
– If it is true what action did the bank take?
– Were the customers so affected notified and rc-imbursed?

3. In how many other branches of the bank did this interest loading take place?
– Did the bank inform the customers in each case?
– Were customers re-imbursed and if not why not?

4. When alerted to these practices what action did senior management take to stop the practices, to inform the customers, and to re-imburse them?

5. Were any managers disciplined for engaging in this practice?

6. How much did this interest loading practice contribute to the bank's profits?

7. When did the interest loading practice stop completely in all branches?

8. RTE has information that NIB imposed extra bank charges on customers without their consent or knowledge. We have documentation which itemises original net fees, the net fee adjusted, and the net fee applied. Our information suggests that in many cases the adjusted fees were not made known to the customers.
– Is this true?
– How widespread was it?
– If the bank was aware of this practice what steps did it take to eradicate it?
– Were customers informed or re-imbursed?
– When did the practice cease in all branches of the bank?
– Were any staff who engaged in this practice disciplined?
– How much did this practice contribute to the bank's profits?

9. RTE has evidence of interest loading on ordinary term loans. This involved altering the agreed interest on such loans without the customers' knowledge.
– Is this true?
– In how many branches did it occur?
– When alerted what actions did NIB take to ensure it could not happen in the future?
– When did it stop?
– Were any officials who engaged in this action disciplined?
– Were customers informed and re-imbursed?
– How much did the practice contribute to the bank's profits?

10. What effect did the Consumer Credit Act have on any of the practices outlined above?

11. What procedures have NIB put in place to ensure that these practices no longer operate?

12. What did NIB now do to re-imburse customers who have been overcharged as a result of these practices?

Yours Sincerely

Charlie Bird
Special Correspondent,
RTE News

George Lee,
Economics Editor,
RTE

Prime Time's executive producer, Eamon O'Connor, also sent a letter to Halpin. He asked for a response to the allegations of loading interest and fee charges. In addition, he wanted to know if customers had been informed or the money given back. The letter from Current Affairs specifically asked the NIB chief to make a spokesperson available to be interviewed for *Prime Time* by 4.00 p.m. on Tuesday, 24 March. With both letters now sent, all that was left to do was wait.

Lee and the *Prime Time* producers gave serious consideration to contacting some of the victims who had been robbed by the bank. They decided against it for a number of reasons. It had only been on the previous Friday that the courts had cleared the way for RTE to contact NIB customers. This allowed a very short period of time to travel to Cork and to Carrick-on-Shannon to explain to the victims what had gone on. In addition, nobody could be sure how these victims would react. It was possible they could libel the bank managers. Things could get unnecessarily complicated. In addition, there was a feeling that the inclusion of victims could introduce an element of overkill into the report.

* * *

The final element of the *Prime Time* report had to be filmed on Tuesday afternoon. The bank had not responded to the request for an interview. Yet the allegations which were about to be broadcast were the most serious ever made against an Irish retail bank. Because of this, *Prime Time* felt it was important for the public to understand that RTE had tried hard to give NIB an opportunity to respond.

At 4.00 in the afternoon, on Tuesday 24 March, Lee drove down to NIB headquarters at Wilton Terrace. There he met Eamon O'Connor and two camera crews. The reporter sat in his car, dialled the bank, and asked to speak to Philip Halpin. He was told that Halpin was not available and that the bank would not provide a spokesperson. One of the camera crews, positioned across the road from his car, filmed this entire phone call.

Ten minutes later, Lee walked into the NIB building and approached the reception desk. One of his television crews followed him in to record the proceedings. The second crew filmed the reception scene from outside the front door.

The NIB receptionist looked up from her desk. She instantly recognised the reporter as he approached. She also observed the camera team who arrived with him. The reporter politely announced who he was, said that he was from *Prime Time*, and asked to speak to the general manager, Frank Brennan. Without missing a beat, the receptionist phoned Brennan's office. She calmly announced that George Lee was in reception and that he wanted to speak to Mr Brennan.

Some minutes later, another young woman arrived down to reception. She walked past the waiting area and began a quiet conversation with the receptionist. The sound recordist had his headphones on and he picked up the conversation on his sensitive recording equipment. He indicated that the young woman had been sent down to get rid of the reporter.

The woman was Frank Brennan's secretary. She was immediately surprised, and visibly unsettled, by the television camera. Lee repeated his request to speak with Mr Brennan but his secretary said that her boss was not available. The reporter then asked if he was in the building, because he would be prepared to wait to speak to him. The secretary said she would not answer that question. Lee pushed a little harder by explaining that *Prime Time* was going to broadcast very serious allegations about the bank shortly. He said that Mr Brennan was aware of that fact and he pleaded for an opportunity to speak to him. The seriousness of the reporter's appeal seemed to register with the secretary. She paused and asked him to wait. Then she disappeared past the security door. Lee sat down again and waited.

Some minutes later, she reaffirmed that Brennan would not be available for interview. The receptionist passed on the message. Lee then asked her if she knew whether or not the general manager was in the building. She said that she did not know. The reporter and his television crew thanked the receptionist and left the NIB building.

On his way back to RTE, Lee received a phone call from Joe Murray, NIB's public relations consultant. Murray was very angry and berated the reporter for invading the NIB headquarters. He said he wanted to register his absolute disgust about the uninvited presence of RTE cameras in the reception area. He accused the reporter of setting a new low for Irish journalism and said the bank would be making a formal complaint about him to the Director General of RTE. The reporter, however, was unruffled. He tried to explain to the PR consultant that he was working towards a *Prime Time* report and that the programme style was different to news. NIB knew what the report would contain but had refused to provide a spokesperson. Very serious allegations were about to be broadcast. The public would have to be aware that these allegations had not been sprung on the bank. The scene at reception would show a serious effort had been made to get a formal response before the allegations were broadcast.

The PR man, however, had no interest in the explanation. He was so angry that he was practically spitting down the phone.

'Are you recording this phone call?' he abruptly demanded.

'No,' said Lee, 'I'm not recording it. I'm driving my car.'

'You're driving your car!' shouted Murray

'Yes. I'm driving back to RTE,' replied Lee.

'Well, I hope you don't crash! I hope you don't crash!' Murray screamed angrily into the phone.

'I'll try not to,' said Lee calmly.

* * *

When he got back to the newsroom, Lee learned that RTE had received a letter from the Central Bank. This letter, dated 24 March, had been delivered by hand earlier that day. Reference was made to the Supreme Court judgment of the previous Friday. It noted the court's recommendation that RTE should co-operate with the regulatory authorities investigating the NIB offshore investment scheme. In this letter, an Assistant Director General of the Central Bank wrote:

> I would be obliged if, to assist the Central Bank in its inquiries, you would furnish to us at an early date, copies of all documentation which RTE has in its possession and on which you rely to support the allegations that have been made about National Irish Bank and its subsidiaries or which suggest irregularities in the conduct of their affairs.

Lee read a copy of the Central Bank letter but didn't think much about it. Neither himself nor Bird would have any objections to such a request for assistance although they would never reveal their sources.

Three hours later, however, the two reporters became suspicious when NIB also quoted the Supreme Court judgment. In a public statement, the bank called on RTE to make the documentation in its possession 'available to the authorities'. Bird and Lee wondered why NIB would make this request at all. Yet, they were even more puzzled that both NIB and the Central Bank could have made the exact same request on the exact same day.

The reporters were excited when they first learned that a new NIB statement was about to be issued. They thought it might contain a response to their latest letter. These hopes were dashed, however, when the press release arrived in RTE by fax at 8.07 that evening. Written in large bold print across the top of the first page was the headline 'NIB CHALLENGES RTE TO PRODUCE EVIDENCE'. The statement said that:

> National Irish Bank has fully considered the judgment of the Supreme Court delivered on Friday last ... The allegations made

by RTE are of a most serious nature and generalise about the practice of the Bank as a whole on the basis of selective information supplied to RTE by disaffected parties ... Although the Bank's internal investigation has found areas which give rise to concern, in fact these sweeping allegations made by RTE have not been substantiated. RTE has refused to make available to the Bank evidence to support its allegations. The Bank now calls on RTE to produce this evidence, either by publishing it or making it available to the authorities, or giving it to the Bank to enable NIB to deal with all of the issues ... This Bank has been pilloried and harassed by RTE on an almost daily basis and its bona fides questioned. The picture painted by RTE does not correspond with the reality of the Bank's policies and practices. The Bank has now been informed by RTE that it will shortly be making new allegations about matters unrelated to CMI which again relates to events which are alleged to have occurred some years ago. It is important that RTE should not neglect to verify its earlier allegations .... The Bank deplores the attacks on the character and professionalism of its staff who are committed to providing the highest service standards to customers.

The reporters viewed the NIB statement as a pointless attempt to undermine their credibility and to deflect them for a while from broadcasting their next story.

* * *

At 10.40 on the following morning, Wednesday, 25 March, National Irish Bank tried once more to deflect the journalists from their report. The new attempt involved a strong letter of complaint to RTE about George Lee. The letter was written by Philip Halpin, NIB's chief operations officer. Halpin demanded that the RTE boss take action against the reporter. He allowed 80 minutes for response after which he said he reserved the right to take the matter further. Halpin's letter read as follows:

> Yesterday an RTE reporter and two crews grossly invaded the privacy of individual staff members of National Irish Bank and our premises. Your employees entered our premises without notice or authorisation and proceeded to harass and intimidate innocent members of staff and to indiscriminately film them in a pressurised environment and in a manner which represented and branded them in an unsavoury fashion.

> We know that the reporter in question was Mr George Lee who has frequently made accusations against NIB. We do not know who the other members of your staff were. This intrusion into the privacy of the Bank follows an ultimatum received from the producer of Prime Time, Mr Eamon O'Connor to make available spokesperson [sic] for the Bank by 4:00pm yesterday. The Bank advised Mr Lee at 4.00 pm yesterday that it would not be making a spokesperson available.

Shortly afterwards our offices were invaded by two crews and Mr Lee.

Innocent members of our staff were traumatised by this experience. To illustrate this I will quote you from statements they have made:

"I was answering a telephone call when I looked up to find George Lee approaching me with two camera men and lights shining in my face. I got an awful fright. Mr Lee asked if a certain senior manager was available. I indicated for him to take a seat. The senior manager' [sic] secretary came down to reception and advised Mr Lee that he (the senior manager) was not available. I advised him that there was no one available for comment. Mr Lee asked if the senior manager was in the building. Again the camera lights were in my face and I again said that I could not comment. I found Mr. Lee's manner to be extremely intimidating and in fact found the whole experience to be intimidating."

"I went to reception to find Mr Lee sitting with a camera and microphone trained on him. I walked behind the cameras and spoke to our receptionist. The camera man indicated to Mr Lee that I was there to speak with him. Immediately the camera and microphone were put in my face and Mr Lee demanded to speak with a senior manager. I informed him that the manager was not available to speak with him. He demanded to know if the manager was on the premises. He also pointed out in the strongest terms that this was a very serious affair which would be the subject of a Prime Time programme very soon. I told Mr Lee that I would return to him. I found Mr Lee's manner to be extremely intimidatory to the point of harassing and feel extremely shaken by the event."

I am advised that RTE has a code which prohibits the invasion of privacy and that this code can only be breached with your authorisation. I cannot see that you would have authorised this type of intimidation and harassment.

I must ask you to ensure that the filming and intimidation of innocent members of our staff is not broadcast by RTE and secondly that disciplinary action be taken against your members of staff.

I must ask you for an apology for this latest bout of unreasonable behaviour by RTE against our Bank.

If we do not hear from you by 12:00 noon today we reserve the right to take further action which may be appropriate.

Yours sincerely,

Philip Halpin

Chief Operating Officer

* * *

Lee read a copy of this letter from the bank shortly after 11.00. The complaint was along the lines he had expected after the phone call he had received from Joe Murray the previous day. He was a bit disappointed that the NIB staff had described him as intimidating. Fortunately, he had camera shots of the event from two different angles. These would prove that his demeanour in the NIB reception area had been far from intimidating.

The reporter was not perturbed by the NIB complaint. It was Wednesday 25 March, the day of the big broadcast and both himself and Bird had other things on their minds. They had been at work from a very early hour going over and over the contents of their reports. Neither of them could think of any more they could do to verify the facts which they were about to reveal. The only thing which could stop them now, would be an order from the High Court. Both of them knew that the bank would not succeed in getting such an order at this late stage. The moment of truth had almost arrived.

Moment of Truth

The reporters spent most of the day putting the final touches to their news report. Annette Kinne finalised the package for *Prime Time*. RTE's lawyers were concerned that the station might be accused of being too hard on the bank. They had considered the eleventh draft of Lee's *Prime Time* script over the weekend. It was the first time they had read through what he was planning to say. His report contained no legal flaws but it was, in their opinion unwise to broadcast it on the night the story was broken. Their recommendation was that the *Prime Time* report should be postponed.

Fortunately for the reporters, the RTE bosses stood firm. They believed the story stood up. Bird and Lee had the evidence, the sources and the documents. RTE would run the story. The lawyers were thanked for their advice but *Prime Time* would go on air as planned.

Bird and Lee had been particularly secretive about what they were working on. Very few in the newsroom knew the details they were about to reveal. Although they could stand over every element of their story, they were still a bit worried that NIB might issue a denial and threaten to sue them. The reporters found it hard to relax, as the final deadline approached, even though no legal challenge had been mounted by the bank.

An eight-minute slot at the top of the bulletin had been assigned for their NIB report. Word spread throughout the newsroom that this latest instalment to the NIB saga would be the most shocking of all.

At 6.01 the last bell of the Angelus was replaced by the low drum roll that signalled the start of *Six One*. The voice of Bryan Dobson boomed out.

'Revealed, how National Irish Bank secretly overcharged some of its customers.'

The newsroom fell silent as everyone waited for the other headlines to pass.

'RTE's continuing investigation into National Irish Bank has uncovered further irregularities,' Dobson came back to the top story.

> The pressure to make profits for the bank created a culture where at certain NIB branches money was taken without any legitimate reason from customer accounts and kept for the bank's own

profits. When the bank became aware of this from its own internal audit reports, RTE's investigations indicate that the vast majority of customers who had this money taken from their accounts were neither told of what had happened nor paid back .... Our investigation was conducted by our Special Correspondent Charlie Bird and our Economics Editor George Lee.

Everybody listened carefully as Bird's voice-over began.

> Former senior employees of the bank have told us that extra charges were imposed on some customers without their knowledge or approval. These claims are supported by other sources and confirmed by internal bank documentation ... Customers were not alerted and no money was repaid and the proceeds went to the bank itself .... Our investigations show at least two separate practices .... The first was increasing or loading the interest on customer overdrafts .... The second was the charging of extra fees on customer accounts without their knowledge or agreement ....

The news report included images of NIB branches, internal documents, and nine different interview clips from the two bankers. It ended with the sign-off, 'Charlie Bird, RTE News at National Irish Bank headquarters in Dublin.'

The silence in the newsroom was replaced by spontaneous applause. The phones began to ring. Viewers from all over the country had been horrified. The government was also shocked. Within an hour, an emergency Cabinet meeting had been called. It was an unprecedented response to a news exposé.

A statement was issued from NIB headquarters at 8.30 in the evening. The bank admitted that customer accounts had been raided. However, NIB used its statement to launch yet another attack on RTE. The bank accused the journalists of allowing themselves to be used by disaffected parties. The NIB statement read as follows:

> The incidents RTE refer to, go back many years and do not reflect the current practices of the bank. Interest loading is not a practice permitted by the bank and the audit reports, which were selectively leaked to RTE, make this clear. This practice occurred in a small number of branches and in a limited number of accounts. It occurred in the late 1980s and early 1990s.

> We accept that customers affected by the unauthorised practice were not advised of it and were not offered recompense at the time. The bank regrets this. NIB will seek to identify such accounts and undertakes to reimburse any customers so affected.

RTE also make allegations regarding extra bank charges. These allegations will be examined fully by the bank. The practices currently followed by NIB are normal industry practice. Charges are fully disclosed and notified to customers in advance.

RTE has again allowed itself to be used by disaffected parties to promote out of date information about the bank in a manner designed to inflict maximum damage on NIB. NIB is gravely concerned that RTE continues to present highly selective information leaked to it to undermine the bank and to misrepresent the bank's management and its staff.'

This NIB statement cut little ice with the government. At 7.00 p.m., exactly an hour after the story was broadcast, a hushed silence descended on the Cabinet room. Bertie Ahern called his meeting to order. Eighty per cent of his ministers were present. They all had been horrified by what they had learned.

The meeting lasted two hours. Then Tánaiste Harney went to the Attorney General's office. Finance minister, Charlie McCreevy, went with her. Central Bank governor, Maurice O'Connell, would join them there. Their job was to finalise strategy. They brought senior Departmental officials. Even their press men tagged along. In the meantime, a holding statement was issued just before 9.30. The government statement spoke of 'grave concern' and 'determination' to see that the money taken from customers would be 'made good by the bank.' The Central Bank, the Garda Fraud Squad, the Director of Consumer Affairs and the Attorney General were all being called in. The forces of the State would come down hard on National Irish Bank.

Five minutes after the government statement was issued, Lee's *Prime Time* report went on air. It was 12 minutes in duration and incorporated a dramatic reconstruction of what had gone on in the bank. The words of the bankers were used, as were images of the documentation they had supplied. The report ended by summing up the seriousness of the situation for the bank.

NIB's marketing literature had traditionally trumpeted the competitiveness of the bank's charges and that they have no hidden costs. Our evidence clearly disputes this. National Irish Bank now faces a number of difficult questions. They're currently embroiled in four official investigations into their controversial offshore investment scheme. And tonight's revelations now mean a lot of new questions need to be answered. This is the first time in the history of Irish banking where evidence has been uncovered that money was secretly taken from certain customer accounts for no legitimate reason.

In the 1980s and early 1990s, National Irish Bank stood out as the most aggressive Irish bank in their pursuit of market share. The result appears to have been a corporate culture which pushed some managers to cut corners and to take illegitimate profits from unsuspecting customers.

National Irish Bank, in their mission statement, say professionalism in their actions and ethics is one of their core values. This is a claim many will demand they live up to in their response to the practices we have revealed – practices which have put the whole Irish banking system in the spotlight.'

* * *

The response to the news and *Prime Time* reports was unprecedented. The RTE switchboard was jammed. Politicians of all persuasions issued statements condemning the bank.' Scandalous' and 'alarming' were the two words most widely used.

An *Irish Times* editorial, published the following morning, captured the mood of the country. Under a heading 'Bad Day for Irish Banking,' the newspaper lashed NIB.

> For the bank to speak of restitution at this point is derisory. Theft and fraud on a considerable scale appear to have been perpetrated. These cannot be other than matters for the Garda and the prosecution authorities.
>
> All over Ireland last night, it cannot be doubted, account holders were drawing down their statements to check figures which hitherto they would have accepted at face value. If National Irish Bank could lard its customers' accounts with unauthorised interest hikes and specious charges, is there anything to guarantee that other banks, or branches, or employees of banks, have not done likewise? Banking is essentially a matter of confidence and that confidence, in turn, is grounded upon assumptions of integrity and honesty on the part of those who staff the institutions. For the great majority of those who do business with the associated banks, last night's allegations must literally belong in the realm of the unthinkable.
>
> NIB has claimed that the alleged malpractices have been discontinued. But the bank's lack of frankness and its unwillingness to square up to unfolding events, leave it with little, if any, credibility. It sought to use the courts, in the first instance, to suppress the findings ... in relation to special investment accounts. It retained consultants to spread the

impression that all was in order and that RTE, in fact, had little of substance to reveal ....

... Somewhere among the employees, or former employees, of NIB, there are also individuals who felt it necessary to break silence on this odious business ...

When Irish banks open for business this morning they will do so in the face of an overall diminution of confidence.

At 11.00 in the morning, on Thursday, 26 March, NIB chairman Alex Spain was summoned to a crisis meeting at the Central Bank. The chief executive of National Australia Bank in Europe, Ross Pinney, and NIB's chief operations officer, Philip Halpin, were summoned along with him. Shortly after the meeting, National Australia Bank issued a statement designed to reassure depositors that their money was safe. Obviously, there was a danger of a run on the bank. NIB customers were closing accounts. If others got worried about the availability of funds, a panic could set in. Don Argus, the group managing director of National Australia Bank, appealed to depositors. It was a statement the Central bank would have insisted upon.

The Australian bank boss said, 'National Irish Bank is part of the National Australia Bank Group, a large global organisation with assets in excess of 202 billion Australian dollars (approximately £100 billion). National Australia Bank fully backs all deposits held at National Irish Bank. All deposits in National Irish Bank are safe and no depositor need have any cause to be concerned.'

The government suspended normal business in the Dáil and allowed two hours for a special emergency debate about the NIB scandal. Opposition politicians who demanded action were pushing an open door.

Taoiseach Bertie Ahern made his position clear. 'The bank must be made accountable. Its customers must be properly compensated and steps must be taken to ensure that the banking system is not tainted by this activity.'

However, it was Tánaiste Mary Harney who stole the show. She had spent the previous night finalising a strategy to deal with NIB and the crisis now gripping the entire Irish banking industry. She was outraged by what had taken place and had no intention of holding back. Shortly after 3.00 in the afternoon, she published a blistering attack on National Irish Bank.

The revelations made last night on the RTE evening news contained the most alarming allegations ever made against a bank here ... disturbing in the extreme ... those responsible for such wrongdoing will be named and treated with the severity which their actions justify .... The Fraud Squad has opened an office this morning .... The Director of Consumer Affairs is carrying out an investigation .... I am making preparations ... to petition the High Court for the appointment of an Inspector ... under section 8 of the Companies Act ... it will be the first time an Inspector has been appointed without a preliminary investigation ... I would like him to establish the nature and extent of the practices ... which customers were involved ... the role played by National Irish Bank management ... were staff disciplined ... why misappropriated funds were not repaid and who was responsible for this decision ... the role, if any, played by the chairman, the directors and members of National Irish Bank in encouraging, condoning, or ignoring the practices .... National Irish Bank is clearly acknowledging that what was contained in the RTE revelations is correct ....

* * *

At 7.50 on the same evening, in response to the hardening of political and public opinion, NIB issued a new statement to the press. This time the bank was much more contrite. Ross Pinney, the managing director of National Australia Bank in Europe, was now 'gravely concerned' at the way NIB customers were treated.

Pinney said, 'it is unacceptable that irregularities uncovered by internal audit reports were not comprehensively dealt with at the time and the customers immediately recompensed.' The statement also announced that Arthur Andersen had been appointed 'to investigate the allegations made against NIB and to establish where reimbursement should be made to customers.'

Mary Harney responded immediately. On behalf of the government, she told the Australian-owned bank that its new apology was 'too little, too late'. Formal complaints from NIB customers had already started to flood in to the Garda Bureau of Fraud Investigation.

* * *

An hour and a half after Ross Pinney's statement, Lee took part in a *Prime Time* studio discussion. Fine Gael Finance Spokesman Michael Noonan also participated in the programme, which considered the public and political reaction to the NIB revelations. In the hospitality room afterwards Noonan casually referred to the speech Charlie McCreevy had delivered in the Dáil that afternoon. He said McCreevy had told the Dáil that the Central Bank governor wrote to him on 19 March. The purpose of this letter was to tell the minister that the Central Bank investigation into NIB's offshore investment scheme had been completed. Lee was shocked. He asked Noonan to repeat what he had just said, which he did. The Fine Gael politician then asked what was wrong.

The reporter explained that the Central Bank had written to RTE on Tuesday 24 March. They had quoted the Supreme Court judgment and asked for copies of all documentation RTE had in its possession relating to the investment scheme. He told how himself and Bird became suspicious when NIB made an identical demand some hours later. Now he was wondering why Central Bank officers would ask RTE for documentation to help them complete an investigation which the government had been told was finished at least five days previously.

Noonan was perplexed but the reporter was disturbed. Although he did not say it, Lee began to wonder what the Central Bank was up to. He decided to get a copy of McCreevy's speech to check it out for himself. It was almost midnight by the time he got to read what McCreevy had told the Dáil that afternoon. The Finance Minister had said that:

> In fact the Governor (of the Central Bank) has already completed an investigation into earlier allegations concerning National Irish Bank. He wrote to me confirming this on 19 March 1998, and confirming again the general satisfaction of the Board of the Bank with the legal framework for bank supervision. I will now read this letter to the House.

> 'Dear Minister,

> I refer to your letter of 26 January requesting a report on the implications, if any for all aspects of banking supervision, of the allegations made against National Irish Bank. I can confirm your understanding that the Central Bank officers who inspected National Irish Bank were acting solely as banking supervisors. Their report is completed ....'

The reporter then looked again at the letter received by RTE, five days later, on 24 March. It said:

> The Central Bank ... is investigating the matters that have been broadcast by Radio Telefis Eireann with respect to that bank [National Irish Bank] ... I would be obliged if, to assist the Central bank in its inquiries, you would furnish to us at an early date, copies of all documentation which RTE has in its possession and on which you rely to support the allegations that have been made ....

Lee phoned the Central Bank press officer at his home after midnight to seek an explanation. He asked him how the Central Bank could tell the Minister for Finance it was finished investigating the offshore scheme and five days later tell RTE the investigation was ongoing. He also asked him if it was pure coincidence that the Central Bank and NIB made the exact same request for documentation from RTE on the exact same day. This conversation between the reporter and the press officer was very heated and lasted for over half an hour. No adequate explanation for the discrepancy between the two Central Bank letters was offered.

* * *

There were no names on the CMI accounts at NIB, only numbers. This was supposed to make them immune from Revenue investigation. Normally the Revenue Commissioners cannot pry into bank accounts unless they know the names of the account holders in advance. This was why so many NIB customers had been willing to trade nine per cent of all their savings for a numbered account. On Friday afternoon of 27 March, however, all that changed.

The Revenue Commissioners let it be known that they had forced NIB to give them full details of all the investors in the offshore scheme. The names, the addresses, and the amounts they put in. The protection and anonymity the investors had paid for was worthless. This came as a surprise to the journalists and it shocked the entire financial community.

NIB had made a fatal mistake in the design of its offshore investment scheme. They had used CMI life assurance policies as a cover for the scheme. However, CMI was classed as a non-resident insurance company. It was based in the Isle of Man, which is not a member of the European Union, and it did not have an office of its own in Ireland in the early 1990s.

Under Irish tax law, the Revenue Commissioners are entitled to seek policy details from any bank acting as an intermediary for a non-resident insurance company. In addition, the Revenue Commissioners are entitled to seek details from an intermediary involved in the transfer of assets abroad, where such transfers cannot be classified as ordinary banking transactions.

It had taken two months for the Revenue Commissioners to convince NIB that these two pieces of legislation entitled them to access the CMI accounts held at the bank.

This success by the Revenue Commissioners had left NIB reeling. The investment product they had sold had been seriously defective.

* * *

Jim Lacey had been chief executive of National Irish Bank from 1988 until 1994. He remained on the board of the bank until September 1997. It was Lacey who had been in charge when the offshore investment scheme was launched. He was also in charge when the internal auditors found that money had been taken from customers in both Carrick-on-Shannon and Carndonagh. When Lacey left the bank in 1994, the government appointed him Chairman of the Irish Aviation Authority. Three years later he was also appointed to the board of the Dublin Docklands Development Authority. In addition, the former banker was chairman of Forum 2000, Fianna Fáil's fund-raising committee. On Friday afternoon, 27 March, less than 48 hours after the new scandal had been revealed, Jim Lacey became the first significant casualty of the NIB affair. He resigned from the two state bodies to which he had been appointed. Lacey issued a statement.

> There have been no allegations of wrongdoing on my part in respect of my former position with the bank. Notwithstanding this, there have been calls by politicians for my resignation from these bodies.

> I do not believe that the interests of these two organisations will be served by me becoming embroiled in a highly charged political debate concerning the bank of which I was formerly chief executive. Nor do I wish to be the subject of a political debate in the Houses of the Oireachtas given my desire for privacy as an ordinary citizen holding no political office. I have therefore decided to resign from these positions. I wish both these organisations every success in the future. I have also resigned from my position as chairman of Forum 2000. I wish to state clearly that my decision today, taken for personal reasons, is not to be interpreted in any way as implying any impropriety by me in my previous role with the bank.

At about the same time as Lacey was falling on his sword, an affidavit on behalf of Tánaiste Mary Harney, was read out in the High Court. The Tánaiste was seeking, and was subsequently granted, permission to apply for the appointment of two High Court inspectors to investigate the affairs of National Irish Bank. Former Supreme Court judge, John Blayney and accountant, Tom Grace, were named as the two inspectors.

The court was told that Martin Cosgrove, the civil servant from the Tánaiste's department, authorised to investigate the NIB offshore investment scheme, had been disturbed by his early findings. Cosgrove had found that NIB did not have proper authorisation for 500 insurance-linked investment policies sold over the previous seven years. According to the authorised officer, the bulk of these policies had been sold to Irish residents and the money involved amounted to £50 million. Cosgrove examined 77 of the investment policies in his first two days and found that 80 per cent of them 'gave cause for regulatory concern'. In 50 per cent of the cases he examined, he found that the money invested 'offshore' had been re-deposited back to National Irish Bank. Officials of his department would soon report 'grave concern that the purpose behind the execution of these policies of insurance may have been to assist customers ... in the avoiding of revenue obligations in this State ... allowing persons to conceal money from the Revenue Authorities.'

With the appointment of two High Court inspectors now inevitable, National Australia Bank decided it was time to talk. A phone call was put through to the Director of News at RTE. Ross Pinney, National Australia's top banker in Europe, offered to be interviewed.

* * *

Bird and Lee had spent the previous two days dealing with the fallout from their story. They had been inundated with phone calls from all over the country. Hundreds of viewers rang to complain about NIB and other financial institutions. Letters arrived from a large cross-section of people. Many of them wanted the reporters to investigate their bank accounts. Some were trying to interest them in new financial stories. Several current and former employees of other banks phoned to tell them that the NIB practices went on in their own financial institutions. The two reporters heard enough stories of scandal to keep them investigating for years.

As well as dealing with all of these phone calls, Bird and Lee had continued reporting about NIB on television and radio. They broadcast every statement that was issued and analysed events as they unfolded. Their workload became very heavy and two personal assistants were assigned to them. Nobody in RTE could remember as big a public reaction to a news story.

It had been a very hectic two days, and Lee, who had been working very late hours, was particularly exhausted. He was preparing to go home before 6.00 for the first time in weeks when Ed Mulhall tapped him on the shoulder.

'I have one more job I want you to do,' he said.

'What is it?'

'An interview.'

'With who?'

'I got a call from the bank. Ross Pinney is ready to talk.'

'They finally caved in.' The reporter was surprised.

'You can take two cameramen, the satellite van and Caroline Bleahen as well. You concentrate on the interview. Caroline will organise everything else.'

'Ironic,' said Lee. 'We repeatedly asked the bank for an interview over the past two months and they always refused. Now that Pinney has agreed I can hardly think of what I should ask him.'

'Just give him lots of opportunities to apologise to customers,' said the Director of News.

A rush of adrenaline revitalised the reporter and he formed a line of questioning. Within minutes he was in his car and heading for the NIB headquarters.

* * *

The receptionist Lee had met on the previous Tuesday greeted him again as he entered the NIB building. She knew he had been invited this time. There was no need to ask why he was there. The receptionist phoned up to the executive suite and announced that RTE had arrived. Then she directed Lee and his team to take the lift up to the top floor.

When they got out of the lift, Lee, news producer Caroline Bleahen and the two cameramen were led into the executive reception area. The reporter took a seat on a couch and waited. The rest of the team busied themselves on the other side of the room.

A few minutes later, Joe Murray, the public relations consultant who advised the bank on its media campaign arrived. Murray is one of the best PR consultants in the country. He is a professional, and usually amiable man. Lee could tell that the PR guru wanted to be pleasant and welcoming this time. However, the strain of the previous two months had left their mark on the journalist. Murray was the very last person in the world he wanted to see.

The PR man sat on the couch and tried to engage the reporter in conversation. Lee was tired and in no mood to put on an act. He could not bring himself to respond. The reporter did not want Joe Murray anywhere near him and he made this clear with his body language. The PR consultant got the message very quickly but he had a job to do. He wanted to give Ross Pinney some idea of the questions that would be asked. He also wanted to lay down some ground rules for the interview. Three times he asked the reporter what he was planning to ask, and three times the reporter refused to answer. 'I'll play it by ear,' was the most elaborate of the responses he gave. Eventually Murray gave up. He walked over to the cameramen who were far more friendly towards him than Lee had been. A few minutes later, the RTE team were led into the office where the interview with Pinney would take place.

* * *

The strain of the crisis was etched on the faces on both Ross Pinney and Philip Halpin. Both men were standing as Murray led the RTE team into the room. Although their mood was not hostile no one could doubt that their humour was grave.

The cameramen set about their work. They positioned two chairs, one for the Australian banker the other for the reporter. Cameras were then trained on each. The few minutes it took to set up the equipment was filled with awkward and insignificant small talk. Murray tried again to get Lee to tell the banker what he would ask.

'Can you give Mr Pinney some idea of the questions?'

'As I told you before, I want to play it by ear. I can't tell him what I will ask, because I don't know what he is going to say.'

'I hope you will be fair to this man.' Murray was smarting.

'This man will get a fair interview,' said Lee.

Thirty seconds later, both cameras were rolling and the reporter launched into the interview. (He stuck rigidly to the line of questioning he had worked out before he arrived.) Pinney performed very well under the circumstances. The Australian came across as an honest, but shocked, banker. He used the interview to deliver the apologies the Director of News had expected.

> We very much regret what has happened to our customers, that it appears that they have been overcharged on fees and interest in this way, and want to get to the bottom of what has happened, and we want to compensate our customers for any wrong doing

that has happened .... There may well be some other branches involved, I don't know, but we will get to the bottom of that, and there will be a complete investigation. The investigation will proceed with speed. I will be asking Arthur Andersen to not look just at the branches that have been identified or the years that have been mentioned, but going through right up until the present time as well.

National Australia group has a strong performance culture. We like to set ourselves stretching but realistic goals, certainly not impossible goals and certainly not ones that lead to this kind of behaviour. That sort of thing is not condoned in any way or tolerated in any way. We like to be competitive in the marketplace but within the principles and the policies that we stand very much behind.

I very much regret that these things have occurred. I share a sense of outrage myself. I am determined to get to the bottom of these things. The National Australia Group deplores the kind of behaviour that has apparently happened. We want to make sure that it doesn't happen again, to sort out the mess, and we want to compensate customers for what has occurred.

Both Murray and Halpin remained in the room throughout the interview with Pinney.

* * *

Minutes after the interview, Murray took Lee into another office to speak with Alex Spain, the chairman of National Irish Bank. Spain, who was in a very emotional and angry state, refused to allow the cameras into his room. He ranted about how he had 'gone out on a limb' to 'raise the standards of internal audits'. He insisted that he had been a 'standard bearer' for audit procedures.

The NIB chairman furiously asserted that he saw absolutely no reason why he should have to resign. He had been chairman of the bank's internal audit committee for nine years, including the years when money was illegitimately taken from customer accounts. Nevertheless, Spain insisted that he never saw any branch audit reports which highlighted the theft.

The chairman also insisted that he had never been aware that the bank's offshore investment scheme was knowingly sold to people who were evading taxes. However, Spain declared on more than one occasion, that his assertions were subject to what he called 'the normal frailty of human recollection'. He added that if it could ever be proven that he was in possession of any such information he would be prepared to reconsider his position on resignation.

The NIB chairman was still in a highly agitated state by the time the RTE reporter left.

The Mop-up Begins

Between them, Ireland's retail banks had 732 branch offices and 183 sub-offices all over the country. It seemed that customer confidence in all of these branches had been shaken. Complaints about all financial institutions flooded in to the Garda Bureau of Fraud Investigation. Not surprisingly, NIB was top of the list. The fraud squad received a total of 119 formal complaints against that bank in just four days. They had a very big job on their hands and they needed to collect information about the practices which had been revealed. Their hope was that Bird and Lee might be able to help them.

A member of the Garda Síochána phoned Bird to discuss the situation. He asked the reporter to meet him and his colleague at 11.00 a.m. in the car park at the university sports centre in Belfield. The reporter chuckled to himself when he heard the location – it was where he met the duffle-bag banker on that wet February afternoon.

Bird was struck by how empty the car park was at that hour of the morning. Two Gardaí sat into his car as soon as he arrived. They broadly described the nature of the complaints they had received and explained that they would be grateful for any assistance. Bird told them he would have to discuss their request with Lee and Mulhall and arranged to meet them again. He emphasised that there was no way either himself or Lee could reveal their sources. Before the Gardaí left, however, they warned him about his mobile telephone. They told him to stop using it and to pass the same message on to Lee.

The Gardaí said ordinary mobile telephones are not suitable for secretive investigative work. Surveillance experts could get copies of the itemised bills for these phones, listing all the numbers which were dialled. This way they could track down the people who were leaking information. Bird was told to get a prepaid 'Ready-To-Go' mobile phone instead, and to tell Lee to do the same. No record is kept of the numbers dialled from prepaid phones. This makes them much more suitable for journalists who want to protect their sources. The reporter noted how emphatic the Gardaí were about their warning. He wondered if they knew something else that they were not telling him.

* * *

Some of the early calls to the RTE newsroom paid off very quickly. One of the NIB bankers who phoned had been grappling with his conscience for years. He said he had worked in a branch of NIB. There, he said, he had participated in all of the practices uncovered by the reporters. Now that the story was out, he seemed keen to talk about what he had done. He invited the reporters to his south Dublin home on the evening of Monday 30 March, and agreed to be interviewed.

This banker said he worked in NIB in the early 1980s as a junior clerk. Two years later, he opened his first bogus non-resident account for a wealthy farmer. The farmer wanted a non-contributory social welfare pension but had too much money to qualify. He asked the bank to transfer his money into an illegitimate non-resident account. This way the Department of Social Welfare could never prove he had money. The state would be tricked into giving him a pension he was not entitled to get.

Like other branches of NIB, the branch jealously guarded its deposit base. There was a constant fear that if customers were not accommodated, they would take their money elsewhere. This would be bad for the branch. The instruction was that no deposit, of any kind, was to be turned away.

The junior official willingly picked the false non-resident address for the farmer. He opted for the one he had seen used most frequently by his colleagues. His fellow NIB bankers openly joked about how many customers the branch had from this place. All of these customers were deceiving the Revenue Commissioners, the Department of Social Welfare, the Health Boards, or other organs of the state.

The bank official pointed out that farmers were by no means the only customers who were assisted in this way: businessmen, hoteliers, publicans and many more. Anybody with a reasonable amount of money, who wanted to dodge their taxes, or cheat the welfare services, would be accommodated. Addresses throughout Northern Ireland, England, and America were easily dreamed up.

About two years after opening his first bogus non-resident account, the junior official was introduced to the practice of loading. He was taught how to extract interest income and bank charges from unsuspecting customers.

The official gave his own description of the fee-loading practice operated by himself and his colleagues:

The smaller, personal fees were left to the more junior members of the staff like me .... There was money to be made in this, but nothing like the money made on the big fees from the commercial customers. It was nearly always done in the evening .... Normally you would get the big fees done in an evening .... The branch ... grew the commercial base ... particularly with publicans or people with supermarkets with big cash turnovers ... where you could afford to load on the fees ... especially with big volumes of cash flow ....That's where the money was to be made ... In the evening we would sit down ... the manager and two assistant managers. I was also brought in .... You would have someone there who was on the cash .... The assistant manager and manager would then have their own opinions about the various customers .... The manager would say 'I think we'll load a particular customer five hundred pounds, what do you think of that' .... Someone else might then say that this customer was a bit of a bastard. The manager might then say 'right then seven hundred and fifty' ... really what you looked at at the end of the day was what happened in the previous quarter ... and if you weren't getting roughly the same amount, or a little more, then you would go back and look at it again. You could load on a bit more here and there where you think you'd get away with it .... The manager might then come back and tell them what other branches had got from fees ... and we may have to look at the fees again. This could go on for two or three nights .... There was great competition between the branches .... Staff were loyal to this particular manager, afterwards they might go for a drink. He was good to the staff, and rewarded them well .... I remember one particular executive, who was transferred from another area. He had never seen these practices before. The first evening he saw them he thought it was a joke, that what they were doing, loading the fees on the customers, that it wasn't for real. By the time of the next charging period this particular person had changed. When someone would mention a figure of five or seven hundred pounds for loading, this guy would say no, and increase the amount further. The manager then laughed and joked and said to this particular person that he'd really got into the swing of things.

* * *

The NIB banker who described the practices was not the only one who wanted to clear his conscience. The following night, Tuesday 31 March, the reporters travelled to Dundalk. There, another ex-NIB banker invited them into his home. This banker gave an even more alarming interview.

He spoke about how he personally had helped a former politician, from a different part of the country, to enrich himself between 1992 and 1994.

The former politicians, who is no longer active in politics, is a successful businessman. He was considered to be an important customer for NIB. The former politician asked the bank to open a false account for him, under the name of Seagull. He was advised, however, that use of this name was unwise. It could draw the attention of the Revenue Commissioners who might want to inspect the account. Also NIB internal auditors could raise questions about it. To avoid these potential problems, the account was opened instead in the name of Charles Gull. The banker described how every weekend during the peak business period he helped the former politician to hide his money.

> I'd make up to four trips every weekend, and wait until maybe four, five, or six o'clock in the morning. Until yer man had counted his money. Then I'd take it back to my branch and lodge it into an account under the name of Mr Charles Gull. I ended up acting like a private Securicor service. He had no security headaches. I took that risk myself for him .... At the end of this strange banking period, the customer would take all of the money out in cash. I don't know what he did with it afterwards, it wasn't my concern, I just hid it for him for the month. I took away as much as sixty thousand pounds in cash each weekend. At the end of the month, the former politician could have anything up to a quarter of a million pounds salted away. He had some payments to make at the end of the period but he took the rest out in cash for himself .... Holding the cash for the month wasn't worth very much. Where it was worth it to me was that we got to provide him with other facilities .... We would do anything to hold onto a good customer.

According to the ex-NIB banker, the former politician ended up with considerable borrowings from National Irish Bank.

* * *

At noon on Wednesday 1 April, Lee queued in the lobby of Kildare House, an overflow facility for the TDs and Senators of the Oireachtas. A large crowd of journalists had turned up to listen to the proceeding of the Joint Oireachtas Committee on Finance and the Public Service. Like the rest of the journalists present, the RTE reporter felt certain that the meeting which was about to take place would be very significant. The TDs and senators who made up the committee had been angered by the RTE revelations. They wanted the organisations responsible for policing Ireland's financial institutions to be called to account. The committee had summoned the Governor of the Central Bank, the chairman of the Revenue Commissioners, and the secretary general of the Department of Finance. All of them had questions to answer as a result of the NIB scandal.

There was a buzz of excitement in the lobby of the building as the journalists jostled for position. Word went around that there was not enough room inside to accommodate everyone. Some of the reporters would have to be disappointed. The waiting journalists began to debate which of their colleagues would be excluded but most of them believed the RTE reporter should be the first allowed in. Lee moved to the top of the queue and got a front-row seat in the visitors' gallery when the journalists were finally ushered in.

Although the bosses of three state institutions were all quizzed by the committee, it was the Governor of the Central Bank, Maurice O'Connell, who bore the main brunt of the questions. O'Connell had issued a written statement to the committee in advance. In it, he pointed out that the primary concern of the Central Bank 'at all times is the protection of the depositors and the stability of the financial system. That is what supervision is about.'

The governor, however, did accept one big problem. 'There is a cross-over point where prudential supervision (of retail banks) ends and what I might describe as consumer protection begins. I have to admit that this is a grey area.'

O'Connell's submission also made it clear that it was the Central Bank who forced National Irish Bank to agree to publish the findings of the Arthur Andersen investigation into the practices RTE had uncovered.

The Central Bank governor, however, did not read out his statement. He had faced this committee before and came away unruffled. Now there was a different atmosphere in the room and he sensed they were going be tougher this time. The TDs and senators were anxious to get going.

Fine Gael finance spokesman Michael Noonan launched into his questions. He asked the governor about the Central Bank's correspondence with RTE, seeking documentation to help complete its investigation into the offshore investment scheme. The governor brushed off his question but Noonan took up the issue a second time.

'When you informed the Minister on 19 March that you had your report completed, why did you get involved in correspondence with RTE subsequent to that and not prior to that?'

'Because I think if we didn't do that,' replied O'Connell, 'we wouldn't be doing our duty. The judgment of the court was that RTE was to co-operate with the other regulators. I think that put the onus on us to go and ask for that information, even if we didn't want it.' The Central Bank governor was nervously tapping his pen on the table.

'But with respect,' said Noonan, 'I'd put it to you that there was an onus on you to do that prior to the completion of the report, not after it.'

'I don't take the point, Deputy, our report was completed before that.'

'Yes, but the allegations were revealed on RTE in the first instance on 23 January. Then the Minister for Finance requested you to investigate and report to him. You reported by way of letter on 19 March, and on 24 March you were writing to RTE looking for information which pertained to the original allegations.'

'And subsequent allegations,' interjected the governor.

'No,' said Noonan. 'The subsequent allegations weren't in the public domain until after your correspondence.'

'We asked them for both,' quipped the governor.

'Then you had information prior to the general public on another set of allegations. Because the dates of your letters would suggest that it was in the interval between your first report and the second set of revelations that you requested the information they had. I cannot understand why you didn't request RTE for that information prior to the completion of your report on 19 March.' The Fine Gael Finance spokesman was determined that he would not be fobbed off.

The governor was becoming increasingly uncomfortable. He began to shift in his chair and the tapping of his pen grew louder.

'That was our judgement and I will stand over it, Deputy.'

'All right,' said Noonan observing the obvious discomfort his questions were causing.

O'Connell repeated himself nervously. 'That was our judgement and I will stand over it.'

'Obviously I am not going to pursue it further,' said Noonan, 'but you didn't answer the question and I wanted to put it to you a second time.'

With the RTE issue now out of the way, Democratic Left finance spokesman, Pat Rabbitte, addressed the governor. He asked if there were circumstances where the Central Bank would revoke the licence of a retail bank.

'Absolutely,' said the governor. 'I think you would rather think in terms first of transferring licences. If you're revoking a licence you're almost at a crisis situation really because, again, I get back to the fundamental point, you're talking about the depositor and what is right for the depositor, and transferring a licence I would suggest to you is a better way of going about it than revoking a licence. I think you can see the point.'

'Thank you,' said Rabbitte.

He had opened the way for more probing questions about NIB's banking licence. Fianna Fáil senator, Michael Finneran, took up the running.

'The NIB has admitted to larceny of some funds, at least, from its customers' accounts,' said Finneran. 'Do you now believe that the NIB have breached the licensing guidelines and regulations as set down by the Central Bank?'

'I am not going to answer a question about NIB,' replied the governor, 'but if any bank is found guilty of larceny in a court of law, it is a very very serious offence.'

'Would it constitute a breach of the licence as given by you?'

'Oh yes, absolutely,' replied O'Connell.

Fianna Fáil TD John Dennehy, then entered the fray. He questioned the governor about the fact that the Central Bank has never inspected a single bank branch in the Republic of Ireland, even though it has always had to power to do so. Dennehy put it to O'Connell that bank customers have no protection.

'We very rarely go into branches,' admitted the governor. 'I don't think that the Central Bank going around and examining every bank branch in the country is the wisest way to go about things.'

'There is a perception that it is done,' asserted the Fianna Fáil TD. 'I think, in the public's mind, they are saying, who is protecting us?'

Fine Gael senator Avril Doyle, had become very annoyed. She narrowed her eyes, and started to wag her finger at the governor.

'Would it be fair,' asked Doyle, 'to deduce from this most interesting and important discussion here today, that the Central Bank has failed the consumer in its supervisory role but it didn't fail the banks in its prudential role?'

'You have been saying that, Senator, and I reject it emphatically.' O'Connell appeared to be struggling to contain his rage.

'Failed the customer but not the banks.' Doyle would not let it drop.

'No! I reject it emphatically, Senator. You have been saying it and I rejected it already.'

'You said you don't investigate the branches because the branches are about customers, so you must have failed the customer.'

'I reject that emphatically.'

'All right,' said Doyle in a mocking tone.

Lee had stayed listening to the proceedings of the Committee for almost two hours. A lot of questions had been put to the governor. By the time he left, the reporter knew that the last short and angry exchange between Senator Doyle and the governor would dominate the News and Current Affairs coverage of the Committee meeting.

In the Shadows

8.00 A.M., THURSDAY, 2 APRIL 1998

Not all of the phone calls to the RTE newsroom proved useful. One of the early callers had demanded to speak with Bird. He made his situation sound serious. The caller said he had some very valuable information which he could not discuss over the phone. It was much too risky. He said he lived in a small village in Carlow and asked the reporter to visit him. Bird, however, was busy and could not go immediately. He learned that Joe O'Brien, the RTE agriculture correspondent, was travelling through the caller's village. He asked O'Brien to stop and check what the man wanted to talk about.

The small terraced house was easy to find. O'Brien knocked at the door. A stout, middle-aged man answered it and ushered the correspondent into his home. He led him to a small living-room containing a bed with a bicycle chained to it. A collection of buffalo heads hung on one wall.

The man said he was an ex-marine and that he had met Elvis Presley at the Newmarket Races in 1979. Elvis, he said, had lodged six million pounds into an Ansbacher deposit account on his behalf. Joe nodded sympathetically and scribbled some notes. The man then spoke of how distraught he had been when he went to the Ansbacher bank and discovered his six million pounds was gone, and that there was no trace of his account. Joe humoured the ex-marine for about half an hour. He promised he would tell Bird and Lee all about the missing money.

* * *

Bird received a call on his car phone from a senior Garda source.

'Charlie, I have some information which I think will interest you.'

'What is it?'

'I'm not going to talk on the phone. Can you meet me?'

'Sure. I'm driving back from Monasterevin right now. I can meet anywhere you like.'

'I can't do it right now. What about this afternoon?'

'Okay so. Where?'

'Garda Headquarters in Phoenix Park. I'll see you in the car park at four.'

'Great. I'll be there.' Bird was delighted. This would be his fourth meeting with members of the Gardaí since the garda had phoned him on Monday morning. He quite enjoyed these meetings because he always came away with some new piece of information.

This time, the information was that Gardaí had received a tip-off. A large shredding machine was to be delivered to NIB on the following Monday morning. They were afraid that someone in the bank might be planning to destroy incriminating documentation. A surveillance operation was planned. The Gardaí were going to follow the delivery lorry to see what was going on. The senior Garda officer thought it would be no harm if an RTE cameraman filmed the delivery.

This was the second time in three days the reporters had been tipped-off about shredding machines being delivered to NIB. Two days previously, Lee had received a call from the press officer at one Government department. The press officer was alarmed because a forty-foot lorry had pulled up outside an NIB branch in Dublin. On that occasion, however, the lorry was long gone by the time Lee and a cameraman had reached the NIB branch, leaving them with nothing to show for their trip.

* * *

On Sunday night, 5 April, a week and a half after the story about 'loading' was broadcast, Bird was watching television at home. It had been a very busy period for himself and Lee. Letters containing details of customer accounts and financial transactions were piling up in the newsroom. It would be difficult to decide which ones to investigate first. This was something both of them would have to resolve over the coming days. Bird sipped a cup of coffee as he watched the television. His mobile phone rang. He picked it up and answered it.

'Is that Charlie Bird?' There was nervousness in the voice.

'It is, yeah. Who's this?'

'You don't know me. I have been watching all that stuff yourself and George Lee have been doing about National Irish Bank.'

'Okay, but what's your name?'

'I can't tell you that, but I think I know someone who might be able to help you.'

'I'm listening.'

'Are you recording this call?' The anonymous caller was still very edgy.

'Of course I'm not recording this call,' said Bird. 'It's Sunday night and I'm at home.'

'Maybe your phone is tapped.'

'It's a GSM phone. They can't be tapped.'

'I don't believe that.'

'Look, you better tell me what you want.' The reporter was concerned that this nervous caller might be a time-waster. However, the fact that the caller had dialled his mobile phone number kept him interested. That number would not have been easy to find. Perhaps one of his many 'Joe McGrath' phone calls was about to pay off.

'I think you might have missed the real story about what was going on at the bank,' said the caller.

'What's that?' asked Bird.

'Fees.'

'We know all about the fees.'

'But it was the main practice. They screwed people for years. It went on all over the place. Yet your reports focused mostly on interest-loading.'

Bird explained to the caller that himself and Lee toned down what they said about fee-loading. He told him that they had computer printouts to prove what had gone on. Two bankers had also confirmed it in interviews. Many more had confirmed it off the record. However, RTE had laid down strict editorial standards. More documentary evidence would be required.

'I think I know someone who might help you to get that,' said the anonymous caller.

'That would be great.'

'Can you get into town tonight?'

'Yes.' Bird got into his car and headed downtown.

'Where are you now?' asked the anonymous caller.

'I'm in O'Connell Street.'

'Okay. I want you to go to Merrion Square. Wait there for a call.'

'Merrion Square? Which side?'

'Near the National Gallery. I'll give you fifteen minutes.'

The phone line went dead again. The prospect of getting more documents had set Bird's pulse racing.

'This is like a film', thought Bird, 'I hope it's not a wild goose chase.'

The reporter arrived at Merrion Square at 10.45 p.m. He had no difficulty parking his car at that hour. It was cold but dry outside, and there were very few people around. Time seemed to pass slowly. Bird checked his phone twice to make sure it was still turned on. Finally, at 10.55, the anonymous caller phoned back.

'Are you at Merrion Square yet?' The banker still sounded tense.

'Yeah. Now what?'

'Walk towards Nassau Street. Stay on the left-hand side of the road. Pass Greene's book shop and continue towards Lincoln Place. You'll come to a public phone box. A few yards past it there is a rubbish bin on a pole. You'll find what you are looking for in there.'

Bird got out of his car, skipped across the street, and walked briskly towards Nassau Street. He looked all around him as he passed the book shop. The street was practically deserted. Bird saw the phone box ahead and, beyond it, the rubbish bin.

Adrenaline took over when he saw the corner of a large brown envelope at the top of the bin.

The reporter glanced in the direction of the dental hospital at Lincoln Place. There, about a hundred yards away in the shadow of a doorway he saw the outline of a man in dark overcoat. The shadowy figure saw Bird looking at him. He turned to his left and disappeared through the darkness towards Westland Row. Bird grabbed the envelope and put it in his inside coat pocket. Then he turned and headed back to his car.

* * *

Back at his home a short while later, the reporter opened the brown envelope. It contained a large number of pages from a computer printout for the NIB branch at College Green. These were different to the printout pages himself and Lee already had in their possession. They contained a much more detailed breakdown of how customer fees and charges were calculated. The most striking thing about the new printout was the extent to which computer-generated fee totals were scribbled out, and replaced with handwritten totals. Bird's analysis of this new evidence was interrupted when his mobile phone rang again at 11.30 p.m.

'Did you get the envelope?'

'Yes. Thanks.'

'That printout will prove how customer fees and charges were increased every quarter to keep them in line with the charges for the previous quarter. What do you think your lawyers will make of that?'

'I don't know,' said Bird. 'Can you get any more?'

'More?'

'Yeah. The more we have, the better our chances of telling the story.'

'I'll see what I can do. I might phone you again.'

'What about telling me your name?'

'You got the envelope, didn't you? My name doesn't matter.'

* * *

Michael Lee, a senior news cameraman, was on duty early on Monday morning, 6 April. He parked his car at the top of the laneway which led to the back entrance to the NIB headquarters. This gave him a clear view of the brown shutter gate which served both as the NIB goods entrance, and as the gate to the car park.

Shortly after 8.00, a large yellow shredding company truck began to reverse down the laneway. The cameraman crept out and hid behind his car. He pressed the record button on his camera and started to film the scene. The big yellow truck came to a halt at the NIB gate. Then the driver hopped out and spoke into an intercom. After a few minutes, the brown gate was partially raised and what looked like a machine was taken from of the back of the lorry. Moments later the gate was closed down and the lorry pulled out of the laneway. The cameraman was very excited by the time he returned to the newsroom.

Bird and Lee were intrigued when they saw what had been captured on tape. They realised that even if a shredding machine had been delivered, it would not mean that evidence was being destroyed. Nevertheless, if the Gardaí verified the delivery, NIB would have to clarify the situation.

The incident with the truck, however, never made it onto the news. The Garda surveillance operation had gone wrong. They had followed the wrong shredding lorry and missed the drop-off at the NIB headquarters.

A few hours after the delivery to the bank, a team of plain clothes detectives called at the NIB headquarters. They asked for an explanation about the delivery lorry. Not long after that, Tom Grace, one of the two

High-Court-appointed inspectors, also called to the bank. The journalists were unable to find out what explanation the bank had offered the detectives. They were also unable to establish if the visit of Tom Grace was in any way related to the incident. Later in the day, NIB denied to RTE that it had taken delivery of a shredding machine.

* * *

Bird was sitting alone in his kitchen at 7.30 p.m. on Monday 6 April when his mobile phone rang. It was a senior Garda.

'Charlie,' he said, 'I have a message for you from my boss. He wants you to know that yourself, George, and your NIB contacts have been under surveillance.'

'Under surveillance?'

'Yeah. There is absolutely no doubt about it. Our information is that two teams of expensive surveillance experts have been employed. Some organisation with very deep pockets has been trying to find out who has been giving you the information about NIB.'

'Jesus. George was right all along.'

'We have our suspicions that an insurance company or a similar organisation may have funded the operation.'

'Why do you think that?'

'We understand that the experts involved are ex-army rangers. They have a particular skill in the use of very sophisticated, high-tech, bugging techniques. These fellows do a lot of work for insurance companies. It could be difficult to link them directly to the bank.'

Bird was stunned. The Ranger wing was the elite force of the Irish army. 'How long has it been going on?' he asked.

'We can't say for sure, but we do know that they have been sticking to you like glue.'

'Have they been spotted?'

'No, but we got a tip-off. I think you'd better tell your colleague immediately.'

Bird looked out his front window as soon as the phone call from the senior garda officer had ended. There was nothing unusual to be seen. He walked out to his back garden and lifted up flower pots. He had no idea what he was doing or what he was looking for. It was like his home had been invaded. He worried about the bankers he had met and the possibility that they may have been seen. The RTE reporter felt angry and sick. He phoned Lee and told him what the garda had said.

Lee was a lot calmer than Bird expected. He had been assuming he was under surveillance for weeks. Lee recalled the incidents on his phone line, his car door being opened, his mother being able to listen in to his telephone conversation. In a peculiar way, he felt reassured by what the garda had said. It suggested his feelings of paranoia had probably been well-founded.

* * *

An hour after the call about surveillance, the anonymous banker phoned back. He said he had more evidence to deliver and told the reporter to drive to St Stephen's Green. This time, the instruction was to park at the Leeson Street end, and to wait for a call. Half an hour later, Bird was sitting in his car, waiting for new instructions when the phone rang again.

'Walk down past the Department of Foreign Affairs until you come to the Irish Bank Officials Association.'

'How far down is that?' Bird interrupted.

'A few hundred yards. There are big granite steps leading up to the door. You'll see a load of empty boxes left out for the bin men. The top box is full of shredded paper. If you look into that you should find what you want.'

Bird did as instructed. A garda stationed outside the Department of Foreign Affairs recognised him as he walked past. This was the quiet side of Stephen's Green but there were still more people around than there had been in Merrion Square the night before.

A hundred and fifty yards beyond the Garda, Bird came across a pile of cardboard boxes. He began to go through them, searching for a large, brown envelope. A woman passed by. She was amused at the sight of the reporter picking through rubbish boxes. Bird, however, was oblivious to her amusement. He could not find the envelope and there was no sign of shredded paper. The reporter began to worry. Maybe it was a set-up. Panic took over and he started to turn the boxes upside down. Then he noticed that they were French wine cartons, not the kind of thing one expects to find outside the offices of the bank official's union. He looked at the name plate on the building. 'The Commons Restaurant'. He had been rummaging through the wrong boxes.

Feeling a bit foolish, Bird walked on for another hundred yards. He came to the offices of the Irish Bank Officials Association. It was the same building that housed the Banker's Club. Four large cardboard boxes had been left beneath the steps for the bin men. He opened the top box and a pile of shredded paper spilled onto his shoes. He dug his hand into the box and was relieved to feel the corner of another large envelope. The reporter paused to examine the contents. It was more computer printouts for the College Green branch of National Irish Bank. He wondered what Lee would make of them. Bird's eyes wandered to the other side of the road. There, in the shadows, standing right up against the railings of Stephen's Green, he spotted the lone figure of a man gazing straight back at him. Neither the coat nor the face were familiar but it was obvious that the reporter was being watched. He stuffed the computer printout back into the envelope.

* * *

The computer printouts delivered by the anonymous caller were very damaging to NIB. They showed in detail how customer fees at the bank's College Green branch were increased for no obvious reason.

Customer names and account numbers as well as their minimum and average balances during the charging period were listed. So also was the number of manual and automatic bank transactions they engaged in. These were totted up to get the gross fee each customer should be charged. An abatement allowance, payable to customers who kept their accounts in credit throughout the charging period, was also listed. This allowance was subtracted from the gross fee to give the net fee chargeable to each customer.

Again and again, however, this computer-generated net fee had been crossed out with marker and a higher fee was scribbled in. In some cases this adjustment merely cancelled out the abatement allowance so that the net fee was adjusted back up to the original gross fee amount. More often, however, the handwritten adjustments went further. In very many cases, the net fee was adjusted up to, and beyond, the amount charged in the previous quarter. All of the handwritten adjustments were initialled by a senior bank official.

Bird and Lee got another of their NIB sources to analyse and explain these new printouts in a filmed interview. Their interviewee was adamant that there was no legitimate reason for the majority of the manual fee adjustments made on the computer printout.

Bird and Lee thought about preparing a new report based on the computer printouts. They discussed the situation with Mulhall. He took the view that the two reporters had already done enough to expose the practices at the bank.

The two High Court inspectors, Blayney and Grace, had been sent into NIB as a direct result of the journalists' work together with the Garda Fraud Squad, the Director of Consumer Affairs, the Central Bank, the Revenue Commissioners, and an officer from the Department of Enterprise and Employment. In addition, Arthur Andersen Consultants had been employed by the bank itself, while National Australia Bank had sent in a top-level audit team.

With so many investigations taking place, the full truth was certain to come out. A new television report from Bird and Lee about fee-loading at NIB would have very little impact at this stage. National Irish Bank had already been disgraced and a revolution in Irish banking had begun.